# Praise for Sandra L. Ceren's books

"...couples can benefit from the extraordinary case studies and quizzes and questionnaires that make up the meat and potatoes of this book. Her books can be read by both the therapist and the clients. Rather than keeping technique and wisdom a secret, she puts everything out in an easy framework so that all can benefit."

—Barbara Becker Holstein, PhD,
Author of *Enchanted Self: A Positive Therapy*

"The case studies dealing with personality disorders and doomed relationships are especially significant in building a long-term relationship resulting in marriage. I particularly appreciated the case studies which illustrated key and lasting, inflexible personality basics that form patterns not easily broken."

—Richard Blake, *Reader Views*

"Drawing upon many years of experience working with couples, Dr. Ceren illuminates essential relationship skills and destructive habits in need of change. Quizzes, real-life stories, and specific scripts facilitate rapid understanding of problems and practical solutions."

—Holly A. Hunt, Ph.D.
Author of *Essentials of Private Practice: Streamlining Costs, Procedures, and Policies for Less Stress*

"Dr. Ceren shares her forty years of experience in helping couples to reduce and prevent relationship problems before committing to marriage. The book is a remarkable roadmap to a healthy relationship and insight into self, written by a therapist who combines experience and skill in improving the lives of others."
—Rosalee G. Weiss, Ph.D., Diplomate,
American Board of Psychological Specialties

## Other Works by Sandra L. Ceren

*Essentials of Premarital Counseling: Creating Compatible Couples (2008)*

*Secrets From the Couch* (2002)

*Prescription For Terror* (1999)

Learn more about Dr. Ceren, read blog postings, and the latest news at www.DrSandraLevyCeren.com

# Look Before You Leap

## a Premarital Guide for Couples

Sandra L. Ceren, PhD.

Library of Congress Cataloging-in-Publication Data
Ceren, Sandra Levy.
Look before you leap : a premarital guide for couples / Sandra
L. Ceren.
    p. cm.
 Includes bibliographical references and index.
 ISBN-13: 978-1-932690-75-0 (trade paper : alk. paper)
 ISBN-10: 1-932690-75-1 (trade paper : alk. paper)
 1. Marriage. 2. Couples--Psychology. I. Title.
 HQ734.C396 2009
 646.7'7--dc22
                     2008036938

Loving Healing Press
5145 Pontiac Trail
Ann Arbor, MI 48105
USA

http://www.LovingHealing.com or
info@LovingHealing.com

Tollfree 888-761-6268
Fax 734-663-6861

Loving Healing Press

# Table of Contents

# 1 What It Takes To Make A Good Marriage

So you're thinking about getting married. If you're a woman, you've probably combed through countless bridal magazines for the perfect dress, but have you really looked carefully to make sure that your intended is as right for you as that designer gown?

Just as you wouldn't buy a car or a house without first doing a little research, you certainly don't want to buy into a marriage before you're sure your partner is the right one for you. You want to avoid a stressful relationship that could nibble away at your self-esteem and cause serous problems along the way. You prefer the nourishment a satisfying marriage can provide.

The wisdom gleaned from many years treating distressed couples led me to develop materials to determine emotional readiness for marriage, compatibility, and willingness to resolve conflicts. These materials, which have been incorporated into this book, contain in-depth personality and relationship quizzes, a list of typical situations couples confront and effective communication and conflict resolution skills applicable to personal and professional life.

Several years ago, over seventy couples seeking pre-marital counseling utilized these materials. Fifty-six couples ranging in age from mid-twenties to mid-forties responded to a five year follow up survey. That the majority of couples returned the survey is significant and beyond expectation. Of the fifty-six couples, forty decided to marry. Thirty-three couples in this group remain in satisfactory marriages (82.5% success rate) They gave excellent ratings to the materials and the counseling experience.

Of the seven remaining couples who married, two divorced and five are in unstable marriages. All regretted not heeding the warning signs. Seven individuals stated they valued the program and materials and used what they had learned to select more appropriate mates.

In the following chapters, you'll find instructions for the quizzes followed by a discussion of significant responses.

Included are a variety of situations that many couples confront. Imagining yourself in the situations presented will help you to learn how you and your partner would likely respond to an actual event. Taking time to review similar occasions in your past will help you discover your coping styles—what worked and what didn't work. You may find a difference in how you'd handle a situation now as compared to how you responded to a similar situation in the past. This reflects your growth.

It takes time to learn if you are suited for one another. Marriages made too hastily may prove risky. Ideally, having time to experience a variety of situations together will be telling. It is time well spent in gathering important information to reflect upon.

From time to time, it is normal for conflict to occur in every relationship. Therefore, using the situations presented in this book, you will attempt to reach mutually agreeable solutions as you practice the conflict resolution skills provided in the chapter.

Occasional arguments or disagreements may be unpleasant, but they are usual and healthy. Two people can't always agree. Asserting a viewpoint is better than closing up and not being oneself. You can offer each other a fresh perspective, as long as you are willing to listen to each other. Heated debates can be intellectually exciting and instructive as long as they don't create chaos and no one plays bully.

Because a "Don't ask" policy does not work in intimate relationships you must share your answers to the quizzes with each other. Sharing your responses to the quizzes can actually create deeper intimacy. Intimates know each other as fully as possible. It's comforting to be understood.

The qualities that help make for a successful union should be considered of primary importance. Identifying them inside yourself will show whether you are emotionally ready for marriage—for a lifetime with that special person in whose company you feel most comfortable.

Opposites may attract. Opposites may compliment, but similarities can provide mutual understanding. For example, it is difficult to complain to someone who is often tardy when you are, too. When two people have similar problems they can support each other in their efforts to overcome them.

Physical attraction, companionship, fear of not finding another mate in the future, motivation to have a family life, or economic improvement are compelling reasons for wanting to marry, but they aren't enough. You want a good marriage, one that provides contentment and stability and allows each of you to reach your own potential, offering comfort when things outside the marriage aren't going well.

People choose to marry for all the wonderful, positive aspects that a marriage can bring. A list of important qualities required for making a good marriage follows below:

## Qualities of a Good Relationship

You must feel safe and satisfied in being together. Pausing to question these feelings may be a warning sign of trouble ahead.

You must be able to share deeply from the heart, to feel truly yourself with your mate, to feel assured that you are accepted as you are, not as someone you pretend to be, or someone your mate imagines you to be, or wants to re-create.

In order to love someone, you must know that person as fully as possible. Each must show that the other's well being is as important as one's own. Love is mutual. It requires picking up the slack without measuring. Love is a quality, not a quantity.

You must share a common value system while keeping an open mind to examine things from your mate's viewpoint

Occasionally, you must be willing to accommodate and grant concessions, providing it doesn't compromise your value system.

A good marriage also depends on an adequate frustration tolerance level. This means a tolerance of your partner's habits or behaviors—some of which may be more or less frustrating depending on your state of mind at that particular moment. For example, when things aren't going well at work or at home or you're feeling out of sorts, your frustration tolerance level can tumble. In other words, a relationship is like a piece of fabric: when one part unravels, it causes more unraveling.

Other qualities that help make for a successful union are detailed throughout this book and illustrated in examples. Identifying qualities within yourself and your prospective spouse will show whether you are emotionally ready for marriage—for a lifetime with that special person in whose company you feel most comfortable

Few couples admit that they would accept a devastating relationship, yet too many accept it as their plight, or their willingness to be martyrs. Based upon clinical observations, at least 15% who stay married would not rate their marriages as satisfactory. Still, many couples enjoy relationships that are a great source of fulfillment, emotional gratification, and comfort.

Grim statistics show that approximately one half of American marriages have ended in divorce. The statistic appears to be going down, perhaps as a result of premarital education. A research project cited in *Family Relationships* reviewed 23 studies on the effectiveness of premarital education and found that the average couple who participated in a premarital counseling or education program reports a significantly stronger marriage than other couples. This book can serve that purpose.

Many people are marrying for the second or third time, repeating their mistakes with other mates who on the surface may appear to be different from their former spouses, but may nevertheless present similar ways of interacting.

Marriage may not be right for everyone. It is important to consider a negative aspect of marriage that some may find too difficult a barrier to overcome.

Living intimately with another person requires making decisions jointly. It means considering another's viewpoint, likes and dislikes, which may differ from yours. This can create stress and shatter an otherwise peaceful existence, robbing you of joy and oft-times, self worth. You must be prepared for a change in lifestyle, one that includes a new set of dynamics and expectations.

Here you will find common sense coupled with forty years of psychological experience and wisdom gleaned from treating couples in troubled relationships. Many of these relationships failed because one or the other of the pair did not know how to read or heed the warning signs. Either their relationship was blinded by unhealthy needs, or they were not ready to commit. When perceptions are clouded by desire, people may overlook important aspects of the person they have chosen for a partner.

Let's take a look at Todd and Jenny, a couple with much in common and an intense physical attraction. On the surface, they appeared to be well matched, and in-love from the start. But was it real love? Real love is sustaining and fulfilling, whereas infatuation is exciting and tentative, a magical chemical wonder that brings a smile to your face and a spring to your step. However, infatuation fades when you're treated poorly by the object of your desire.

## Todd and Jenny

Todd and Jenny, in their late-twenties, met at a church singles social and were instantly attracted to each other. They shared the same religious and ethnic background, and enjoyed sailing and water sports. They were ambitious and had complementary successful sales careers. Todd's in real estate and Jenny's in mortgages.

They longed for each other and could hardly wait to be together, so when Jenny's furnished apartment sublease ended they decided to live together in Todd's fashionable condo. Jenny offered to pay Todd rent and her portion of the utilities, but he refused. However, he accepted her offer to pay for their lavish meals in trendy restaurants and stocking the refrigerator with his favorite foods.

They regarded this period as a trial marriage. At first, it felt like a honeymoon, falling asleep in each other's arms and waking up contented, but soon Jenny tired of Todd's frequent reminders that they were living in his house that he had worked hard to purchase.

Jenny loved to cook and made spectacular meals, but Todd wouldn't allow her to crowd her cookware inside his cupboard. "You have no right to add your kitchen stuff to my house," he snapped.

That he only allowed a small portion of the hall closet for her clothes and insufficient space for her personal items added to the stress of living in his house under his terms. She told Todd that if he really loved her, he wouldn't be so selfish. He ignored her comment

Todd's investment in his independence and his unwillingness to share showed Jenny his lack of consideration for her feelings and diminished her feelings for him. The guy who had made her heart pound, was now making her stomach turn. He refused to attend couples counseling. "It's my way or the highway," he claimed.

Despite all they had in common, age, jobs, family backgrounds, religion, interests, and an intense physical attraction, this relationship couldn't work. Todd proved himself unready for marriage. Jenny left him and bought her own condo.

Two years later, she reported she was engaged to a "quality guy" who knew how to express his love for her as she did with him. She plans to rent out her condo and buy a house with her husband.

Through mutual friends, she learned that shortly after she'd left Todd, he had a six-month marriage that ended in divorce.

It is important to be on the alert when you're infatuated and eager to marry because your intense feelings may tend to take over and you may overlook important characteristics of each other. You may attribute certain valued qualities to your intended, because these qualities are what you'd like your mate to have, but you need proof before facing the challenges and impact marriage will inevitably have on your life.

Despite high divorce statistics, many couples rush into marriage adding to the grim statistics. They don't stop to figure out why their previous marriage didn't work, and how to make the next one better.

Others enjoy emotionally gratifying marriages because they had good evidence of what they were getting into.

Let's look at Brad and Emily. Despite an eighteen-year age difference, this couple was right for each other.

### Brad and Emily

Brad and Emily met at a foreign policy lecture at the university. He was a twenty-seven year old doctoral candidate in the chemistry department and Emily, at forty-six was a history professor. During the Q and A, Brad asked many of the questions that Emily had on her mind. She agreed with all his points. After the lecture ended, they discussed the content in greater depth until the room was empty and they were asked to leave. They continued their conversation over coffee at a nearby café. This was the start of a long friendship based on a commonality of interests and viewpoints.

Brad and Emily would frequently meet between classes to plan support of a political candidate. The rapport between them gave them a special bond. Often, they seemed to know what the other thought and felt. They enjoyed hiking and biking and spent their free time together over several months.

It wasn't until Emily had a serious bike accident and was incapacitated that they realized how deeply they felt for each other. Brad took care of Emily and she let him know that she was grateful. He was the kindest, most thoughtful person she had known.

Brad's tenderness revived feelings Emily hadn't experienced since she was a hot-to-trot young adult.

She found Brad intellectually and emotionally mature, with the vigor and passion expected of a young man.

Brad had dated many women his own age, but he considered them immature and was tired of what he considered silly dating games. With Emily it was different. He felt in complete harmony with her. They fell in love—for all the right reasons.

After two years, they decided to get married. At first Brad's parents disapproved because they wanted grandchildren, but they respected Brad's carefully considered decisions. Brad and Emily enjoyed a full life and didn't want the responsibility of parenthood.

Brad and Emily will soon celebrate their twenty-fifth wedding anniversary. They are best friends, allowing each other freedom and independence to pursue their own creative pursuits. Brad is a serious photographer and Emily, an accomplished sculptor.

A disparity in ages may be a barrier for other couples, but for Brad, emotionally mature beyond his years, and Emily, youthful and vibrant for her age it made no difference.

Let's meet Jim, the infidel, and Rhonda, a naïve woman.

### Jim and Rhonda

Rhonda and Jim worked for an advertising agency and assigned to the same project. They spent many hours side by side enjoying the creative challenge the work demanded. Soon they became pals, sharing personal information. "After two years, my marriage is stale. Boring," Jim said. "We argue about having kids. I don't want any. Sometimes I wish I were single."

"Single, huh? Well, the grass is always greener," Rhonda admitted. At thirty-five, she was tired of the single scene. Enjoying Jim's attention, Rhonda looked forward to the time they spent together at work. She admired his artistic flair and regarded him as a sophisticated, mature man of forty from whom she could learn. She saw no harm in being attracted to him. It wasn't as if he were a happily married man, she reasoned.

Soon, they took a few extended lunch hours to walk on the beach. One day, they held hands. Rhonda felt a tingle surge through her. Aroused, she pulled him close to her and kissed him. Thus began a torrid love affair that ultimately claimed his marriage.

Rhonda made no attempt to learn why Jim had found his marriage stale and boring, nor did she find out whether he wanted children in his future.

Soon after his divorce, Jim and Rhonda married. Concerned about her biological clock, Rhonda discontinued birth control without consulting Jim. Within a few months she was pregnant. Complications confined her to bed requiring a leave of absence from work.

Jim's attention to Rhonda dwindled. He showed no compassion for her situation and refused to do any household chores or make her comfortable in any way. He spent weekends skiing or sailing—leaving bed-ridden Rhonda entirely on her own.

He began to come home from work later and later. When she questioned him about his project, he became angry. "I didn't tell you to get pregnant. I don't want any part of this. I want out. I'm involved with someone else."

Upset and crying uncontrollably for several days, her pregnancy problem worsened and she suffered a miscarriage. Her grief over the loss of her baby and her husband pushed her into psychotherapy.

Rhonda learned that she had projected her own needs on Jim, assuming he would delight and accept their baby because she wanted it, and that he would be faithful because she wanted him to be. She had deluded herself. She hadn't seen him clearly and had chosen poorly. She should have listened when a divorced friend had recommended pre-marital education.

Blinded by passion, and an urgency to marry, she hadn't considered that since Jim was unfaithful to his first wife, he could also be unfaithful to her. Only later did she learn that he had been married twice before his marriage to her. Each of those brief marriages ended in divorce due to his infidelity and selfishness.

Rhonda realized that Jim was fickle, untrustworthy and immature and not the man she had imagined him to be. She realized too late that she should have taken a closer look at him, and considered that he said from the beginning that he didn't want children.

She vowed in the future, she would stop, look, listen and evaluate. Rhonda learned a tough, but valuable lesson.

Let's take a look at Josh and Abby, an ideal successfully married couple in their mid 30s. It's a heartwarming story with many obstacles few could have navigated so successfully.

### Josh and Abby

A recent arrival to town, Abby's life as a single was remarkably unimpressive until she hooked up at a reception for tenants of the office building where she worked as marketing director.

Josh was an engineer and everything her past boyfriends weren't. He was honest and fair. He had a great sense of humor, enjoyed visiting interesting places to take photographs, and above all, he was sensitive and intelligent and treated her with respect. Abby was attracted to him, but she held herself back because there was a major drawback; he had recently separated from his wife, a dangerous woman with a serious personality disorder, and Josh had full custody of his young children to whom he was very attached. She figured Josh wasn't marriage material, but she was eager to have him for a friend as they shared the same values. And so began a two year relationship that culminated in a glorious wedding.

Josh and Abby had taken time to get to know each other well by the time they had set a date. They had pre-marital counseling and attended parenting classes designed for divorced parents.

Abby hadn't met the children until almost a year through the courtship. She was introduced as Dad's friend. The children saw her as an easy-going warm person, and readily took to her. Josh and Abby agreed that the children would come first in his life.

For the children's sake, she hadn't slept in Josh's bed until after they remodeled and re-furnished his home to their mutual tastes and were married. On occasion she slept in the downstairs guestroom, while the family slept upstairs, as when Josh had an emer-

gency appendectomy; or when one of the children
was ill, and she stayed over to help.

Abby and Josh made agreements regarding the
role she would play as a mother-substitute. A highly
sensible young woman, she instinctively knew how to
handle normal conflicts with children. If she and
Josh weren't in agreement, she deferred to "Dad."
They plan to have more children.

Abby and Josh represent a couple who took time to
know each other and found they could handle conflicts together reasonably well. Abby accepted that
coming second to the children was worth the price to
have Josh for her husband. Not everyone could do
that, but so far, it's worked out exceptionally well for
this family.

Although some couples have had the good fortune
of entering into a marriage after a brief courtship, it
is risky and therefore not recommended. It is much
better to allow enough time to know each other as
well as possible to avoid unpleasant surprises.

Many relationships fail because one or both partners do not know how to read or to heed the warning
signs, or their relationship was blinded by unhealthy
needs, or they weren't ready to commit. An important
quality for any human being is a high level of tolerance especially when living with another person.

## Frustration Tolerance

If you and your mate have low frustration tolerance, please consider your relationship as a bumpy
road requiring frequent work. Be alert to the fact that
it is better to assume a "wait and see" approach before taking the plunge. Time will tell if you are willing
and able to take on the task. Love may not be enough

to maintain your tolerance, as witnessed by troubled couples.

If at least one of you has a high frustration tolerance, imagine that person as a tank capable of riding a bumpy road without much difficulty, but remember that even an iron clad tank can break down without proper care. Even the most tolerant person can ultimately lose patience. Typically, this results in an explosion out of proportion to the triggering event. Also consider that having a "high frustration tolerance" may be a disguise for being a martyr, or a feeling of low self-worth meaning such people feel they have to put up with unpleasantness from others because otherwise they will be alone.

## Doubts

If you experience unremitting doubts about a pending marriage, it is urgent that you examine the doubts. Are they based on a negative experience with your prospective life partner? What did that person do or neglect to do to cause your concern? Give full attention to the event or events that gave rise to the current uncertainty that the chosen mate may not be appropriate for you.

- Set aside uninterrupted time to discuss it with your partner.
- Keep an open mind.
- Take time to digest and reflect on the answer.
- Does the response clear the doubt?
- Is it something you can live with and feel confident that it won't return to haunt the relationship?

- Are you the kind of person who can forgive and forget? Do you have a history of storing grudges?

- Do you save another person's mistakes for future ammunition?

A one-time forgiveness pass, depending on the seriousness of the matter, may not be difficult to issue, but repeated bad behavior shouldn't be tolerated. It will destroy your good feelings for your mate and your self-worth.

## Indecision

If indecision is a chronic problem that occurs in many areas of your life, then naturally it will be especially difficult for you to commit to a critical, life-altering decision such as marriage. Indecision can stem from insecurity—a lack of trust in self-judgment, or a wish to be perfect. Often indecisive people can make excellent decisions for other people, but not for themselves. The fear of making a mistake prevents them from moving forward. Becoming aware of this characteristic may be a first step towards the process of changing. Consider the case of Kelly and Ivan:

### Kelly and Ivan

Ivan and Kelly met in their senior year at their state university. They enjoyed the same activities, shared the same values and became best friends. After graduation they went in different directions to attend graduate school, and kept in touch for several years while dating others, admitting their preference for each other. When they returned to their hometown, they dated one another exclusively for five years, but Ivan had difficulty making the decision to marry. He believed his indecision had nothing to do with Kelly, but was due to his traumatic childhood before his parents' divorce. He didn't want to reproduce their life. Kelly could not reassure him that she and he were different from his parents. She wanted a family and her biological clock was ticking. Her ultimate decision to terminate the relationship failed to stir him. A few years later, she married someone else.

Upon receiving Kelly's wedding announcement, Ivan felt devastated and berated himself for his indecision. He became depressed. He realized that his indecision had paralyzed his career opportunities and social life. Ivan had dated a few women, but no one came up to his standards. Afraid to make the wrong decision, he made no important ones. Anxiety had paralyzed him. Now, in his late forties he decided to seek therapy to improve his life.

## Sometimes It's Better to Delay

Many people wait too long to determine if their upcoming marriage is right for them. Despite serious conflicts, some couples resist delaying a wedding. They think that the money already spent shouldn't be wasted. They fret over the embarrassment a postponement would cause them and their families. They sincerely hope a few counseling sessions will clear up their conflicts, or that their problems will simply vanish after the stress of the wedding is over. However, the tendency to overlook potential problems early on is dangerous. These problems will not evaporate, but will probably loom large in the future. Becoming aware of these problems may steer you towards psychotherapy before committing to a marriage. The cost is far less than the cost of delaying a wedding. A divorce would be much more expensive financially and emotionally than the cost of the most lavish wedding and honeymoon.

While some individuals are emotionally troubled, not all are motivated to seek treatment. Some are uncomfortable with the expectation that they will be asked to reveal their innermost feelings or thoughts. To do so, they run the risk of feeling ashamed, misunderstood, or rejected as damaged goods. They do not realize that a well-respected psychotherapist would be non-threatening, understanding, compassionate, empathetic and beneficial. A loving, supportive partner can offer encouragement and would appreciate the payoff.

## You Can't Change Your Partner

Would you buy a beautiful pair of shoes that may look great with all your outfits, but they pinch and will probably causes blisters? Do you hope that the shoes can be stretched to fit your feet? Unfortunately this rarely works. The shoes must feel comfortable when you walk a distance in them and shouldn't require any major adjustment. However, if all that is required for your comfort is the removal of a buckle or a loose thread and the shoes feel wonderful, then that's a deal.

Stay with the shoe analogy a bit more. You really love those shoes. You can't stop thinking about them. They're eye-catching, but no matter how many ways the store has tried; they can't fix the shoes to fit your feet. Would you have foot surgery to make your feet fit the shoes? Surely, not. You'd find another pair, maybe not as attractive, but comfortable.

I am reminded of a man who asked his fiancée to change her hair color to red. Reluctantly, she agreed, but the color didn't go well with her complexion. Despite her discomfort, he insisted she keep it. When he suggested she have breast enlargement surgery, which she didn't want, she ended the relationship. Her integrity wouldn't allow her to re-create herself to become his fantasy love-object. She wanted to be loved for her own qualities.

In the throes of passion and a desire to marry, you may be prone to overlook important personality characteristics. You may attribute certain valued qualities to your mate because these qualities are what you like your mate to possess, but you need evidence. The quizzes will help you dig for the treasure that may or may not exist.

The intrigue, the mystery hidden in another person may be exciting, but it can also be fraught with danger.

### Serge and Suzie

Serge dazzled Suzie with his continental charm, his debonair manner, his impeccable attire and his attentiveness. He took her to the finest restaurants and venues, often arriving with a small gift to delight her. He reminded her of her father. When she was a young child her father would return from a business trip with a small gift for her. She treasured those gifts.

Serge was readily affectionate and she was physically attracted to him. She enjoyed his company

much more than she had with any other man. After a
blissful year filled with expensive weekend trips to interesting places, they decided to buy a house and
move in together before setting a wedding date. It
wasn't until then that Suzie asked about his previous
relationships—a subject that they oddly had not visited in the year they were dating. Serge told her his
wife was killed in an accident several years ago in
Russia before he left for the States. He claimed he
had no children. Suzie was respectful of his reluc-
tance to discuss his past.

Serge found a beautiful expensive house and refused Suzie's share of the cost, stating he had sufficient cash to pay for it. Suzie was stunned at the
huge wad of money Serge produced from his pockets.
She became suspicious and questioned him about
where that much money came from. He told her he
won it at the racetrack. When she asked him about
paying taxes on his winnings, he glared at her shouting, "None of your business." This was the start of
their first and last argument. When she attempted to
question him further, he lurched at her and nearly
strangled her before letting go. Terrified, she ran
away. Soon after her traumatic situation with Serge,
she changed her phone service.

Suzie realized that Serge's life was a mystery to
her. She had fallen for him based on superficial
things such as his nonchalant spending style, his expensive clothes and car and surprise gifts to her, all
of which had initially impressed her. Despite the material pleasures Serge had provided, Suzie realized he
wouldn't have been a worthy husband. His violent
temper frightened her. He appeared to be hiding im-

portant information from her. When they had first met, he mentioned that he was an importer, but she had neglected to ask about the products he imported. For all she knew, Serge could have been involved in something dangerous. She shuddered to think she could have been caught up in that.

The horrifying incident taught Suzie not to rely on superficial niceties, and to take a closer look at the men she dated.

It is important to keep in mind that you can't force someone to change. He must first recognize a better payoff for himself if he changed some of his long-standing behavior patterns, and he must be willing to work hard at it. You can support his efforts, but there's no guarantee of permanent results. Remember this mantra:

"I'm not a tailor, and you're not a garment."

| | | |
|---|---|---|
| **2** | **Personality Quiz** | |

Many of us wear rose colored glasses when looking at our loved ones or ourselves. The quiz is only valuable after you trade the rose colored glasses for a high powered magnifying lens. Consider the quiz the start of your journey towards self-discovery.

On your voyage you may find qualities that make you proud. You may also find some negative qualities. After all, no one is perfect, but you're evolving. Every day we learn new things about the world and about ourselves. You may realize there are some changes you'd like to make—not just for your mate, but for yourself. This is a good sign. You must be motivated and able to see the advantages, the value of making your life better. Change takes time-time well spent because you must live with yourself every where you go for the rest of your life. You must like who you are. Taking care of your physical and emotional health is your responsibility and shows maturity. Several roads lead to personal growth. You will find professionally recommended self-improvement books and other tools listed in the Resource section.

## Supplies

Each of you will need a pen and a three-ring binder to accommodate at least 50 pages.

On a copier or scanner print two copies of each quiz from this book—one copy for each of you to store in the binder.

## Instructions

To achieve the best results you must be willing to explore your inner world with honesty.

Choose a comfortable, quiet place where you can be alone without interruption.

Take as much time and page space as necessary to copy each question and reflect on it. It may help to close your eyes before answering.

Use an ink pen to write down the first answer that comes to mind. A good relationship depends on your honesty. You want to be loved for who you really are, even with your imperfections—everyone has some. Don't change your answers to appear more desirable. The "real" you is bound to surface at some point. Better now than later. Marriage is challenging. It's the beginning of a new lifestyle with different dynamics and expectations. Are you ready?

After quizzes are completed, make one copy of each completed quiz to exchange with each other.

Let's set sail on this voyage of discovery.

**Personality Quiz**

1. Are you satisfied with yourself?

2. What do you like about yourself?

3. Have others told you that they admired those qualities, too?

4. What would you like to change about yourself?

5. How often do you think about the past?

6. What are your feelings about your past?

7. Do you blame others for things that go wrong in your life?

8. Are you lonely when you're alone?

9. Do you often feel sorry for yourself?

10. Do you prefer being alone, or with others?

11. Are you satisfied with your career?

12. Do you change jobs often? Explain.

13. Do you keep good friends over many years?

14. Do you have bad habits that are difficult to break?

15. Do you get angry quickly and lash out in unpredictable ways?

16. Must you always be right?

17. Do you pay close attention when someone is telling you how he feels? Can you put yourself in that person's shoes?

18. How do you usually respond when someone shares feelings with you?

19. Have you been in trouble with the law?

20. Were you ever in debt or bankrupt?

21. Do you have good credit?

22. Do you have frequent nightmares?

23. How often do you get high or drunk?

24. Can you delay gratification? (Can you save the candy bar for later?)

25. Do you make quick decisions?

26. Do you have a difficult time making decisions?

27. Do you spend money impulsively?

28. Do you substitute excuses for explanations to avoid responsibilities?

29. Do you own a personal gun or other weapons? If so, why?

30. How would colleagues and friends describe you?

31. What is the longest time you have been on a job?

32. What are your career objectives?

33. If you could do anything you wanted, what would you do?

34. Describe your personality.

35. Have you consulted a mental health professional? Why?

36. What did you learn about yourself?

37. How many marriages have you had and at what ages?

38. How long did they last?

39. Why didn't they last? Be specific.

40. What have you learned about yourself from past relationships?

41. How long did you know your current mate before considering marriage?

42. How are you suited to each other?

43. How are you different?

44. What do you like about your mate?

45. How often do you mention it?

46. What don't you like about your mate?

47. Do you mention it? How often?

48. Do you think your mate is holding something back from you?

49. Do you think your mate understands you?

50. At what age was your first sexual experience?

51. With whom?

52. How did you feel about it later on?

53. List any current sexual concerns.

54. Do you think it's okay to lie in certain instances? Give examples.

55. Describe the personality of each member in your immediate family, their ages, and your relationship with each. Take as much space as necessary.

56. List your past and current problems with your family.

57. Are you religious? What faith?

58. How do you feel about your mate's religious preference?

59. Do you want children?

60. How will you decide their religion?

61. Is it necessary that you both keep the same faith?

62. How many pregnancies have you had or been responsible for?

63. Abortions?

64. What street drugs have you used?

65. If you have stopped, how long ago was that?

66. Are you still drawn to any drugs?

67. Describe your appetite for food.

68. Describe your sexual appetite.

69. What are your sexual fantasies and fetishes?

70. Are you easily frustrated?

71. Do you think some people are out to get you?

72. Has anyone suggested you're too critical or fussy?

73. Do you agree with others' perceptions of you?

74. Are your feelings easily hurt?

75. Have you been accused of playing rough?

76. Do you think you and your partner are sexually compatible?

77. Do you consider yourself a team player? Explain.

78. Are you an independent thinker or do you go with what is popular?

79. Do you express your viewpoints adequately?

80. What would you do if you found a wallet or purse?

81. Your neighbor is a hothead. His wife screams, "Help." What do you do?

82. How do you handle insults?

83. At a checkout counter, a clerk makes a mistake in your favor. What do you do?

84. At a shopping mall you see a child being beaten. What do you do?

85. Have you had suicidal thoughts? When? What precipitated it? What prevented it?

86. Did you have a plan?

87. Have you ever been unfaithful to someone with whom you were involved?

88. How did you feel about it?

89. Do you have annual physical checkups?

90. Do you have any physical complaints that you don't address?

91. Do you practice safe sex?

92. If you had a sexually transmitted disease, would you tell your partner?

93. Have you suffered from anxiety or depression? How frequently? When? How was it treated?

94. Have you seen or heard something that you knew wasn't real?

95. What are your hobbies and interests?

96. Describe any unusual past experiences.

97. What is your favorite activity?

98. Are you comfortable sharing your feelings about most matters with your mate?

99. Do you prefer to keep your feelings to yourself?

100. Do you feel understood by others?

To interpret your responses, read them as though a stranger wrote them.
- Would you like that person for a friend?
- Exchange the pages with your partner. Consider your partner's responses.
- Are they more similar or different from yours?

- Have you discovered something new about your partner?
- Does it change your feelings about committing to that person?

| **3** | **Discussion of Responses to Personality Quiz** | |
|:---:|:---:|:---:|

### 1. Are you satisfied with yourself?

Answering in the negative shows honesty. Many people are not completely satisfied with themselves. They recognize that there is room for improvement.

If you feel truly satisfied with yourself, either you among the most fortunate who have evolved to his potential, or you do not recognize your faults, or simply accept them. Accepting yourself may be a positive quality, as long as friends and associates have no serious complaints about you.

### 2. What do you like about yourself?

Hopefully, more than two good qualities are listed. If not, either you are too hard on yourself, or you don't appreciate yourself sufficiently. You may be expecting too much of yourself. Your self-esteem may need a boost.

### 3. Have others told you that they admired those qualities, too?

If so, you have validation, a substantial reason to feel good about yourself.

If not, then you may not see yourself clearly, or you may not have heard the applause.

### 4. What would you like to change about yourself?

Does the desire to change come from your partner's complaint? Do you agree? If you don't agree, or aren't motivated because you think it will take too much effort, this is likely to be a source of friction and should be resolved before you take the relationship further. However, if you've arrived at this decision independently, it is a goal you can accomplish with your partner's support and encouragement.

For example, if you would like to lose weight or to firm up, you can do it if you're willing to exercise at least three times a week and maintain healthy eating habits.

Smokers, drinkers, gamblers and those with other addictive behaviors often respond to self-help groups using the typical twelve-steps (Alcoholics Anonymous) format. The key to change must start with you. Support comes from others.

Sometimes it may take a medical emergency to propel someone to change an addictive behavior. Others are so hooked that they ignore the serious consequences of their addiction. I knew a woman with emphysema who could not quit smoking even after she had to use a breathing machine. She hobbled around with the cumbersome oxygen apparatus and continued to smoke. Her husband, her children, and her friends pleaded with her to quit. Her physician repeatedly cautioned her about the grave consequences to her health. A friend gave her a gift of a series of hypnosis sessions. She willingly submitted to the sessions, but alas, her smoking addiction won out. She died at fifty-five years old. If she had tried to stop smoking early on, it might not have been so difficult for her. This true story shows the overwhelming power of addiction.

It is best to stop when you first become aware of your grim habit before it is too late.

If you would like to change a bad habit, such as procrastination, you can, but only if you are motivated. Ask yourself what you would gain if you didn't procrastinate. Some people proclaim they would welcome the relief from the stress caused by procrastination. Others admit they actually enjoy the rush of adrenaline as they hurry to meet a deadline. They work better under pressure; steered by adrenaline, their senses become more acute. Which type are you?

### 5.  How often do you think about the past?

Some people dwell on the past with regret and remorse for not taking the opportunities presented or for the mistakes they may have made, or for the hurt they may have caused. "If only, I had made a different choice in school, career, place of residence, or relationships."

Thinking about the past in this particular way is not helpful. It is better to use the past in a constructive way—to learn from it. How did we come to make the decisions we made? What propelled us toward our choices? Did we take into consideration all the information available? Was there something we overlooked? If we considered all the information available at that time, then what seemed appropriate and good then, may simply have not turned out the way we expected through no fault of ours. We aren't prophets and can't predict the future. It is useless to kick yourself in the backside for something that wasn't your fault.

What we learn from our past decision making process can help us use these lessons to our advantage. If you are the type of person who quickly jumps to conclusions without taking into consideration all the available information, then you've learned a valuable lesson. Now that you are aware of this aspect of your personality, you can prevent yourself from jumping to conclusions again.

Thinking about the past with nostalgia brings memories that can nourish you. Dwelling on the past, however, prevents you from moving forward.

### 6.   What are your feelings about your past?

Anger, regret, disappointment? Learn from the situations that caused these feelings, but don't dwell on them because that will have a negative impact on your mood.

Joyful moments should be relived. They sustain us. They make unpleasant times less so. For example, when imprisoned in the dental chair, your mouth full of annoying dental gadgets, not knowing how long the unpleasantness may last is an ideal time to conjure up past pleasurable scenes. Close your eyes and picture one of the most picturesque places you've visited. The Swiss Alps, the Maui beach, wherever. Making believe you are there instead of the dental chair or other unpleasant place can make the present situation feel less unpleasant.

### 7.   Do you blame others for things that go wrong in your life?

If you answered in the affirmative, this is not a good sign. Apart from the times you acted on misinformation or poor advice, you must accept some responsibility for most things that go wrong in your life. The key is learning to accept responsibility where pertinent and not shift it on to others.

### 8. Are you lonely when you are alone?

If you answered in the affirmative, it probably means that you are too dependent on others for amusement, or support. You may not have developed adequate interests or activities that challenge or excite you when you are alone.

When you were a child you may have enjoyed the stimulation of siblings or an extended family around you much of the time. Now, you may have to tap into your own resourcefulness. Some people are afraid to be alone, because they anticipate unpleasant thoughts. When they are alone, they may ruminate about negative things. If this is true for you, it is an area worthy of exploration.

### 9. Do you often feel sorry for yourself?

If this is true, please examine your reasons. Are they legitimate?

### 10. Do you prefer being alone or with others?

If you prefer being alone than with others, imagine how you would feel sharing your daily life with a partner. If your partner also prefers being alone than with others, you may be able to create a mutually beneficial arrangement. You can respect and accept your partner's need for solitude, yet enjoy your time together. The trick is timing. Hopefully, you will want to be together at the same time. If not, can you compromise? If your partner does not respect your need for solitude and wants constant togetherness, she may not be an appropriate partner for you.

### 11. Are you satisfied with your career?

You may be unsure how to answer this question. Ambivalence is not so terrible. You may need to find new goals. Your dissatisfaction may not be about your specific career, but the place or people with whom you are working. You can explore this issue with someone familiar with your situation, perhaps a trusted, savvy colleague.

If the place or the people with whom you are working are not causing dissatisfaction, but the kind of work itself, you can seek a change. Consider career counseling. Many state colleges and junior colleges offer free, or low cost vocational counseling to residents.

### 12. Do you change jobs often? Explain

Changing jobs frequently when presented with a better opportunity (which you've carefully evaluated) may be a positive sign. It shows you are unafraid of making changes to improve your situation. However, changing jobs often because of discontent with your job certainly deserves further examination. It suggests emotional instability and may be a sign that you aren't ready to commit.

### 13. Do you keep good friends over many years?

If you and your long time friends value each other, it is a good sign.

### 14. Do you have bad habits that are difficult to break?

If your mate repeatedly complains about these habits, and you make no effort to change, it may jeopardize your future together, especially if this involves self-destructive behavior such substance abuse, gambling or other addictions.

**15. Do you get angry quickly and lash out in unpredictable ways?**

If this is true, you are not ready for a healthy relationship.

**16. Must you always be right?**

If so, you will be a difficult partner unless your partner is very tolerant.

**17. Do you pay close attention when someone is telling you how he feels? Can you put yourself in that person's shoes?**

"Yes" means you are a sensitive person with a desirable personality quality that should serve you well in your relationships. It would be best to have a partner who shares this quality. If your partner does not, you must be willing to make adjustments and accept her for her other qualities. As you know, no one is perfect.

**18. How do you usually respond when someone tells you how she feels?**

Ignoring her feelings, or telling her she shouldn't feel that way, is not helpful and can push her away.

Listening to her and telling her that you want to understand will show her you care. Offering unsolicited advice, although well intend may fall on unappreciative ears.

### 19.  Have you been in trouble with the law?

Explain any past incidents in which you have had trouble with the law.

### 20.  Were you ever in debt or bankrupt?

If yes, a full disclosure to your partner is in order. Debt, depending on the circumstances, usually shows a lack of responsibility and an inability to delay gratification. Hopefully, this was a long time ago and you no longer are in debt, otherwise, you must tend to this matter as soon as possible. Until your financial affairs are approaching order, a permanent relationship may be risky.

### 21.  Do you have good credit?

Do you have a history of bad credit? You must disclose and explain it.

### 22.  Do you have frequent nightmares?

If your nightmares are recent and you have not experienced post-traumatic stress, the cause of your nightmares should be explored with a health professional. They may be a result of your fear of commitment.

### 23.  How often do you get high or drunk?

Getting high or drunk makes you a risky partner. The more frequent, the riskier.

### 24.  Can you delay gratification? (Can you save the candy bar for later?)

Difficulty in delaying gratification suggests immaturity. When you give in to immediate gratification, you miss the thrill of longing. You miss the anticipation for something you desire. Try delaying gratification to build up your anticipation. You may find the excitement of waiting prolongs the thrill.

### 25. Do you make quick decisions?

If you do not take the time to examine all aspects of your decision, but act impulsively, this is not a good sign.

### 26. Do you have a difficult time making decisions?

Indecision can keep you from moving forward. It may mean you don't trust yourself to choose wisely, or that you are a pessimist expecting your decision to result in a disaster of some kind. This particular trait, by itself may annoy you and your mate, but it may not destroy a good relationship.

### 27. Do you spend money impulsively?

Unless you have unlimited wealth, impulsive spending can destroy a relationship. You must be willing to consider your partner's opinion on big ticket purchases. If you proceed with an expensive purchase against your partner's opinion, your relationship may be headed for trouble.

### 28. Do you substitute excuses for explanations to avoid responsibilities?

This is an undesirable trait. Admitting responsibility for your action or inaction is more acceptable than making excuses.

### 29. Do you own a personal gun or other weapons? If so, why?

Often people who feel the need for a personal gun are insecure and fearful of their environment. Do you have this fear?

If you own a personal weapon, you must discuss this with your mate. She must feel comfortable with it. If she does not and you insist upon keeping your weapon, your relationship must be reconsidered.

### 30. How would colleagues and friends describe you?

If they say good things about you, you and your mate should be delighted.

If they say unpleasant things about you, make an effort to understand their comments. Accept responsibility. Figure out the reasons for your behavior and if you are willing, you may see the value in changing.

### 31. What is the longest time you have been on a job?

Depending on the length of your work history, less than six months suggests a problem.

### 32. What are your career objectives?

Having career goals is a positive sign.

If you have no goals because you are satisfied with your work, this isn't a problem

If you feel stuck and have no clear career goals, a career counselor may help.

### 33. If you could do anything you wanted, what would you do?

Don't ignore your passion. Explore ways of getting there, perhaps as a sideline. Some doctors write medical thrillers. Some mathematicians are sculptors.

Some teachers are performing artists. The list goes on.

**34. Describe your personality.**

**35. Have you consulted a mental health professional? Why?**

**36. What did you learn about yourself?**

**37. How many marriages have you had and at what ages?**

**38. If so, how long did they last?**

Brief marriages may imply that you didn't know each other well enough before marriage.

**39. If so, why didn't they last? Be specific**

If you have had two or more marriages and have not had individual counseling, consider doing so before marriage.

**40. What have you learned about yourself from past relationships?**

**41. How long did you know your current mate before considering marriage?**

Less than one year is insufficient. Hasty marriages are risky. It is important to spend adequate time together in a variety situations, to feel comfortable in speaking openly about yourselves, to learn what each of you expect from marriage, to understand your partner's worldview. It is important to ask questions to listen and digest before committing.

**42. How are you suited to each other?**

People with similar values and hopes are usually more likely to understand and appreciate each other.

### 43.  How are you different?

Differences can be exciting and challenging, but if your values conflict, it predicts trouble ahead. Consider that it is very difficult to change each other's values. It is easy to give lip service in order to make peace, but if it isn't genuine you will be living a lie. In order to enjoy and benefit emotionally from a marriage, you must be truly yourself.

### 44.  What do you like about your partner?

If you list fewer than four items, either you are overlooking something, or he isn't the right one for you.

### 45.  How often do you mention your partner's good qualities?

Saying something you appreciate about each other at least once a day helps to nourish the relationship.

### 46.  What don't you like about him/her?

If you answered "nothing" you are probably overlooking something since nobody is perfect, but it does suggest you are satisfied with your mate.

If you've listed several items, decide if you can tolerate these things long run.

### 47.  Do you mention your partner's negative characteristics? How often?

Do you refrain from discussing things that annoy you, hoping they will go away, or are too uncomfortable to make waves? If so, you must take the initiative, and put it to your partner in a constructive way; for example, "You probably don't realize it, but when we're out with other couples, it annoys me when you interrupt me. I'd appreciate you're not doing that. Maybe it would help if I gave you a signal. I could cough or scratch my ear. What do you suggest?"

If on the other hand, despite your frequent and intense comments about your partner's disturbing behavior there has been no change, you may need to find a softer approach. If this doesn't work, remember you cannot change her. You are not a tailor and she isn't a garment.

**48. Do you think your mate is holding something back from you?**

If this is true, it is a red flag. Check it out immediately.

**49. Do you think your mate understands you?**

If you answered NO, this is a red flag.

**50. At what age was your first sexual experience?**

**51. With whom?**

**52. How did you feel about it later on?**

**53. List any current sexual concerns.**

**54. Do you think it is okay to lie in certain instances? Give examples.**

**55. Describe the personality of each member in your immediate family, their ages, and your relationship with each.**

**56. List your past and current problems with your family.**

**57. Are you religious? What faith?**

**58. How do you feel about your mate's religious preference?**

**59. Do you want children?**

You must both feel the same way about whether to raise a family or not. Attempts to convince your partner to go along with your choice may cause trouble in the future. You must be in agreement on this important issue which will change your whole life. Once you become a parent, you are a parent for the rest of your life.

**60. How will you decide your children's religion?**

You must be in agreement on the choice of your children's religion and respectful of your partner's religion if different from yours. Some parents expose their children to different faiths allowing the child to decide. This may not be the best approach because it can create conflict and confusion for the children. They may find it difficult to choose between their mother or father's faith because it involves showing favor towards one parent over the other.

**61. Is it necessary that you both keep the same faith?**

It may not be necessary that you keep the same faith, but you must be comfortable with any decision you make in this regard.

**62. How many pregnancies have you had or been responsible for?**

**63. Abortions?**

**64. What street drugs have you used?**

**65. How long ago did you stop?**

**66. Are you still drawn to any drugs?**

**67. Describe your appetite for food.**

**68. Describe your sexual appetite.**

Some relationships fail because of a vast difference between sexual libido. If this is a problem for you, you must be willing to accommodate. This means you won't always get or give what you desire. If you demand that your sexual needs are met but your partner's libido is not as high as yours, the relationship is in trouble.

**69. What are your sexual fetishes?**

As long as your fetishes are not offensive to your mate and they do not cause any harm to anyone, you can enjoy a healthy sex life together.

**70. Are you easily frustrated?**

If your mate is tolerant of this aspect of your personality, it may play an insignificant role in your relationship.

**71. Do you think some people are out to get you?**

If you have concrete evidence that this is so, you must share this with your mate.

If you have no proof, but you have a strong feeling that others are out to hurt you, this must be addressed in individual counseling before you commit to a permanent relationship.

### 72. Has anyone suggested you are too critical or fussy?

If more than one person has suggested it, it is probably true. Decide if you want to change this behavior. It may not ruin your relationship, but it will make it difficult, depending on the tolerance level of your mate.

### 73. Do you agree with others perceptions of you?

Your agreement shows you are open-minded. This is a good quality.

### 74. Are your feelings easily hurt for yourself and others?

"Yes" shows you are a sensitive person, perhaps highly sensitive, and passionate. This means you can appreciate the nuances in situations. Sensitive people often appreciate the arts: music, drama, art, literature, film, etc. Although your sensitivity causes you emotional hurt, if it allows you to feel for others as well, it can be a positive quality. It can propel you towards helping society.

### 75. Have you been accused of playing rough?

Have you lost your temper and assaulted someone? Explain the circumstances and how you control your impulses now.

## 76. Do you think you and your partner are sexually compatible?

If not, are you sure you are prepared to accommodate? How important is sex to you and your mate? Some couples do not rank sexual compatibility as very high on their list. Other values take precedence. A thirty-five year old man said, "Oh, sure I'd love to have more sex, but my wife is so good to me in other ways, that I accommodate. When she's too tired, I take care of my own sexual needs. I know she loves me, and that is enough."

## 77. Do you consider yourself a team player? Explain

There are several ways to look at this issue. In order to be a team player, you must go along with what others do at the workplace or in social situations. This may mean compromising your values. You must define your priorities and act accordingly. While being a team player is valued in the workplace, one must examine the cost. Recent corporate scandals are a perfect example.

Whistle-blowers are courageous for standing up for what they believe is right. They pay a high price for calling attention to the wrongs in the corporate world. They risk losing their jobs and being ostracized by their colleagues. They believe expressing their values and being true to them are worth the negative fallout.

Going along with things you don't believe in, just to be accepted or to keep a job defines you as a person. Check where your mate stands in this regard.

If your mate wants you to be a team player, but it goes against your grain, this may not be a deal breaker, but it can cause problems. Once again, it shows the importance of sharing the same values.

### 78. Are you an independent thinker or do you go with what is popular?

(Read above) It's always better if you and your mate see eye to eye on this.

### 79. Do you express your viewpoints adequately?

If not, and you are willing, you can improve your communication skill.

### 80. What would you do if you found a wallet or purse?

Consider how you would feel if you lost your wallet or purse. Wouldn't you want someone to return it to you? If you cannot put yourself in that person's place, you are missing an important quality that most people would prefer to have in their mate. If you made every effort to find the owner, but couldn't, would you consider giving the money to charity? Would you and your partner handle this situation similarly? Would it pose a problem in the relationship if you each handled the matter differently?

### 81. Your neighbor is a hot-head. His wife screams, "Help." What do you do?

Ignoring a plea for help, indicates you are a selfish human being and would make a poor mate. An appropriate response would be to call 911 and report the situation immediately making sure law enforcement takes it seriously. You can ask the dispatcher to withhold your name.

### 82. How do you handle insults?

In the heat of anger you may retaliate and ignite a battle you may not win. It is better to put aside the insult or criticism when first made, and deal with it after you are calm. The person who insulted you may need better communication skills. He may not have meant to insult you, but he was too harsh. You can reframe the insult into a constructive criticism and if you judge it to have any merit, you can learn from it, choosing to accept it as a gift. If after the passage of time, you see no merit to his remarks, consider the source as someone jealous of your achievements.

### 83. At a check-out counter, the clerk makes a mistake in your favor. What do you do?

If you do nothing, and feel good about it, you may have a bit of larceny in your character.

If your mate would call the clerk's attention to the error and you disagree, you are not well suited to each other. Honesty is a core value couples must share.

### 84. You see a child being beaten. What do you do?

If you don't attempt to stop the fight, or call 911, you are too self-involved and would not make a good partner.

### 85. Have you had suicidal thoughts? When? What precipitated it? What prevented it?

If these thoughts are current, please see a mental health professional immediately.

### 86.  Did you have a plan?

If you are not currently suicidal, but have been in the past, watch for symptoms of depression and if they occur, immediately seek help.

### 87.  Have you ever been unfaithful to someone with whom you were involved?

If you have a history of infidelity, you are a marriage risk.

### 88.  How did you feel about it?

### 89.  Do you have annual physical check-ups?

Taking care of your health is your responsibility. It shows maturity.

### 90.  Do you have any physical complaints that you don't address?

If this is true, examine your reasons for avoiding medical attention. It is better to address this issue before marriage.

### 91.  Do you practice safe sex?

If not, you are a risky partner.

### 92.  If you had a sexually transmitted disease would you tell your partner?

If you don't, you show a lack of consideration for your partner and are a poor risk.

### 93.  Have you suffered from anxiety or depression? How frequent? When? How was it treated?

Full disclosure to your mate of your physical and mental health is imperative.

## 94. Have you seen or heard something that you knew wasn't real?

Visual and auditory hallucinations should be discussed with a psychiatrist.

## 95. What are your hobbies and interests?

If, according to your partner, you spend an inordinate amount of time on these activities, you must both reach a satisfactory compromise to avoid friction later.

## 96. Describe any unusual past experiences.

Please elaborate. When sharing this with your mate, please answer his questions truthfully. Full disclosure is important for an intimate, healthy union.

## 97. What is your favorite activity?

Will this activity take you away from your mate for prolonged periods? Marriage requires compromise. Each couple should have individual time to themselves, or else they can suffocate each other. Golf widows complain about their husband's absences, but they rarely divorce because of it.

## 98. Are you comfortable talking about how you feel about most matters with your mate?

A healthy relationship requires the freedom to talk about most matters with each other.

## 99. Do you prefer to keep your feelings to yourself?

If you do, then you are not taking advantage of the emotional support you can gain from sharing your feelings with your mate. If you are ashamed of your feelings, you must examine your reasons.

A handsome, young married patient had sexual fantasies about his flirtatious women colleagues. He loved his wife and their new baby and would not jeopardize his family by giving in to his flagrant sexual opportunities. His wife was totally involved with the care and feeding of their infant and as most new mothers, she was physically exhausted and her libido was diminished. Her husband understood and respected her feelings. His arousal in the company of flirtatious women disturbed him and he decided to tell his wife about it. She said she appreciated his honesty and knew he would not betray her. Sharing his feelings with her placed a shield around his desire, holding it in check keeping the couple's emotional intimacy strong. Their open discussion led to a renewed sexual awakening for her not too long afterwards.

## 100. Do you feel understood by others?

If you feel you are an open book, you have nothing to hide. Good for you!

If you feel others do not understand you, cite specific situations where this has occurred. Are you evasive? Do you find communication difficult? It is most important that your mate understands you. If she doesn't, this is a bad sign. Emotional intimacy re-

quires understanding and accepting the other person—as is.

| 4 | Relationship Quiz | |
|---|---|---|

## Instructions

- Do this in a quiet place, alone without interruption, allowing sufficient time away from your partner.

- After you and your partner have concluded the quiz, arrange to meet to exchange pages.

- Do not read your partner's responses until you are alone and have uninterrupted time to read, digest, reflect.

- When you are ready, make a list of points to discuss at your next meeting.

1. Give examples to show how you and your mate handle stress, frustration and dilemmas with friends, family, and at work?

2. How do you show compassion and affection?

3. Do you laugh and cry at the same things?

4. Are you competitive or cooperative?

5. What evidence do you have to show that you can depend on your mate in emergencies?

6. In what ways does your mate add or take away from you?

7. Are your separate personal goals compatible with those of your mate?

8. Are you assured you can trust and respect each other in all areas of life? Give examples.

9.  What evidence do you have that you work well together?

10. Do you share the same ethics, values, hopes and dreams for your future together? Elaborate.

11. Do you agree on large financial expenditures, savings and investments that impact your shared lives?

12. Does it matter who makes more money or who has a more prestigious job?

13. Do you have similar spending styles? If one is thrifty and the other has a lavish spending style, arguments are inevitable and issues of control will surface.

14. Are you willing to budget to determine if certain expenditures are affordable and then behave responsibly?

15. Have you established if you want children or not or whether you are in agreement in being undecided? Or how long to wait before trying to conceive?

16. Should you have children will you both take parenting classes and share in parenting?

17. If you have been married before, what have you learned from the experience?

18. In what ways is your current partner similar and different from former significant others?

19. If your prospective mate has similar personality characteristics to someone in your

family, please explain. Do you get along well with that person?

20. If you have different religions, are you willing to respect the differences and to agree on the religion in which to raise your children? Deciding to wait until after you marry to make this determination sounds a warning bell.

21. Are you willing to admit mistakes and to make appropriate amends?

22. What evidence do you have to show that you listen to another person's point of view and your willingness to compromise?

23. Give examples showing the circumstances to which you have accommodated.

24. What have others said about your ability to communicate and share your thoughts and ideas?

25. Are you concerned that your partner may be keeping important information from you?

26. If you haven't asked about this, why not?

27. What opinions of your mate have your friends and family expressed?

28. Must you always be right? Or must you always give in?

29. How do you and your potential spouse handle conflicts? Do you compromise or does one of you give in? How do you feel about each other and yourselves afterwards?

30. Name three things that make you angry?

31. How do you express anger?

32. Name three things that make you sad?

33. How do you express sadness?

34. Name three things that make you smile.

35. Do you experience yourself and your mate as physically appealing?

36. How do you feel when your mate pays attention to a member of the opposite sex?

37. Who decides on the entertainment?

38. Do you enjoy the same entertainment?

39. Do you like your mate's friends?

40. Do you feel respect for your mate?

41. Do you feel respected by your mate?

42. Do you need time to pursue your interests without your mate?

43. How does your partner feel about this?

44. Does your mate spend too much time with friends or at a recreational activity without you?

45. At times do you feel suffocated by your partner?

46. Is there a mystery surrounding your partner you want to solve?

47. What are you planning to do about it?

48. Do you look forward in being together?

49. How often do you quarrel?

50. What do you quarrel about?

51. How do you make up?

52. Are you comfortable with your partner's family?

53. How do you feel about your partner's career choice?

54. Are there times when you are ashamed of your mate? Explain

55. What aspects of your partner do you disapprove?

56. What aspects excite you or make you proud?

57. Does your mate pay you appropriate compliments?

58. What would you like from your mate that is missing?

It is not necessary for all answers to be positive in order to enjoy a successful marriage.

For example: Many good marriages are not always built on strong physical attraction. Although sexual passion enhances the union, it can create a smoke screen. Emotional conflicts can erode sexual desire. The person who made your heart pound has the capacity to make your blood boil.

You do not have to perceive and respond to situations similarly in order for you to enjoy a good relationship, but it is important that you make an effort to understand and respect each other's feelings, although different from yours. This requires a willingness to see things from your partner's point of view.

Marriage requires an adjustment to your independence. You and your mate will have expectations of each other. You must determine if they are acceptable to you. To make a satisfying marriage, you must design your marriage together based on a new set of acceptable expectations that can change during different stages in life. Mutual understanding may take some time, but when you value the relationship, it is worth it. You can apply this understanding to other relationships in your life, i.e. your co-workers, friends, family members. Understanding the viewpoints and feelings of others helps you navigate your world better

It is important to remember that good marriages require intimacy—the intimacy of best friends and to have a best friend, one must be a best friend.

| 5 | Communication and Conflict Resolution | |
|---|---|---|

Communication is the key to an intimate relationship and is often presented as a couple's major problem.

The good news is that communication skills can be learned and applied given patience and dedication to the common goals of preservation and betterment of your relationship. Good partners must be willing to discard their old communication styles in favor of a new style, one with proven success. The tools learned have an added benefit: They can be used in other interpersonal situations.

Conflict occurs in all relationships because no two people, no matter how loving, how close, can always feel, think and agree at all times. They are not clones.

Couples must learn that it is important early in the relationship to make a pact to communicate openly and honestly about matters of mutual concern. Holding on to grudges is unfair to the relationship and is a sure-fire way to erode intimacy.

Learning the art of gracious compromise can thwart arguments and lead to mutual satisfaction. A willingness to make gracious compromises demonstrates each individual's contribution to the betterment of an intimate relationship. However, when one grudgingly make compromises, it takes away from the potential of the relationship. This doesn't mean you should do something that upsets you just to get along with your partner. It simply means that you are willing to agree to do something that is not your first choice.

For example, let's say it is Friday evening and you've agreed to dine out. You're feeling tired after an exhausting work week and you'd prefer to dine at a local Chinese restaurant, but your mate doesn't particularly enjoy that cuisine. He urges you to try a new bistro an hour away. You try to explain that you are tired, but your mate convinces you that he will drive and you can rest during the trip. Somewhat reluctantly, you agree, but when you arrive at the new venue, it is very crowded and there is a long wait for a table. You are weary and hungry and feel justified in your anger and you punish him by refusing to talk to him.

Yours was not a gracious compromise. You had a choice and you agreed to go along with him. Perhaps assertiveness is not your strong suit, but you can learn the technique of self-assertion when you realize you deserve to discuss your preferences.

To punish your partner by your silence compounds the bad feelings you both had over your respective decisions. A better compromise would have been to stick to your point that you were tired and wanted to stay closer to home and to ask him to pick a place he would find acceptable nearby—not necessarily the Chinese restaurant. You could have also recommended that you go the bistro of his choice over the weekend after you were rested.

### Jen and Jim

Jen and Jim wanted to go the movies, but they couldn't agree over their choice of a film. Finally, Jen gave in to Jim's choice. Though he was pleased to get his way, his pleasure was short-lived. On the way to the theatre, Jen became unpleasant and resentful and this continued all through each violent scene on the screen. It turned out Jim realized his pick was a poor one, but Jen didn't give him a chance to explain and to agree as she continued to berate him afterwards as well.

Jim felt frustrated that she wouldn't stop berating him, and wouldn't stop for a moment to allow him to express his opinion. As her tirade escalated, Jim grew silent. By the time they arrived home, Jen had quieted. Jim said, "If you didn't want to go to the movie, you should've said so."

"I wanted to please you," Jen replied.

"But if you had told me that you really didn't like my choice, I'd have accepted it and we'd have found a different movie."

"I can't tolerate all that blood and guts. It's revolting."

"Not to me. If you don't like what I like and you think it's disgusting, next time, don't agree to do something you don't want to do and then make me pay for it."

It wasn't until the next morning that the couple's anger subsided. Such is the legacy of grudgingly given compromises. Hence, next time you agree to compromise, make sure that it is really okay with you. If it isn't, the outcome will probably not be a positive one.

Does that mean that you should give up on compromising? Or that everything should be done your way? Of course not! What it does mean is that you need to learn how to compromise graciously. Here is how you can make that happen:

Explain what you want, but also listen with an open mind to what the other person prefers.

Give careful consideration to the other person's wish as a viable option. Be fair. Don't just judge it as ridiculous without giving it serious thought.

Be open to alternatives other than your first choice. Regard second or third choices that may be acceptable to both parties.

If the choice is difficult to make, leave the decision to chance. Write each choice on separate scraps of paper and place them in a basket or a bowl. Let your partner blindly pick one.

Why does it have to be a movie, or a sporting event, or a concert? If you can't find entertainment that both of you can agree on, think about how else you might spend the evening.

Be open to serendipity- discovering pleasurable things by accident. Sometimes someone doesn't expect to enjoy something but it turns out to be wonderful. An art gallery opening reception for an artist's works can be a delightful way to spend time together, pointing out to each other what you especially like about each work of art. Experiment by listening to different types of music to see if you can find pleasure in the same things. Bowling may be a new sport for you or your mate and you may enjoy it.

Gracious compromises may take more time and effort than grudgingly given compromises, but the end result will be well worth it.

The following are some typical complaints of couples:

## "He doesn't listen to me"

If you characteristically approach a topic in a negative way, blaming your mate for not fulfilling your expectation especially when he wasn't made aware of it, he probably won't want to listen to you. For example:

> "Didn't you listen when I said I'd like to go to that new restaurant? Why didn't you make a reservation for Saturday?" or "You should have made a reservation."

Consider a different style of communicating:

> "I'm a little disappointed because I'd hoped you'd have made a reservation for Saturday night at that new restaurant we were talking about the other day."

When you approach the subject this way, you are taking responsibility for your disappointment, and your mate would have no reason to complain that you expect him to read your mind.

He is more likely to say, "I wish that you'd have reminded me. I'll try to make a reservation now, and if I can't, how about next Saturday night?"

## "You don't understand me.""You never validate my feelings. You tell me I shouldn't feel that way, but I can't help the way I feel. You act like I have no right to my feelings."

If you are the recipient of such comments, and you want an emotionally fulfilling relationship, it's vital that you eliminate words that build a wall between you and your partner. To your way of thinking, the person shouldn't feel a certain way, but the reality is one can't prevent the arrival of one's feelings. We are not responsible for our feelings, but only for the actions we take because of them.

We are entitled to our feelings—no matter what they are. They should be acknowledged and respected.

Imagine yourself in her situation. How would you feel? If you have a tough hide, this task may be difficult for you. If you think she is too sensitive remind yourself that hypersensitivity isn't her fault. It's the way she is made.

In any case, a good response would be: "I'm sorry you feel this way. Is there anything I can do to help?"

This shows acknowledgement and respect for your mate's feelings, and that you are on the same team.

**"She always complains. She gets angry at me for reasons I don't understand."**

It may well be your partner has unrealistic expectations of you and these must be addressed:

"Let's talk about your gripe. Tell me what I
did wrong and I'll try to fix it."

If you don't agree about the reason for the gripe, you can say, "I don't believe what I did was entirely wrong. But I can see you're upset. Tell me more about what's troubling you, so I can fully understand."

You may disagree with your mate, but show her, you are trying to understand her viewpoint.

Enlighten the other person about what bothers you.

"I get hurt when you speak to me angrily.
You may think there's nothing wrong with it,
but it feels patronizing to me."

Suggest another way to phrase what he said that hurt you: "If I do something that you don't like, please tell me in a reasonable tone. I don't like when you yell at me to pick up after myself. It upsets me when you call me a slob. When you do that, I feel like you're my father, and I'm a bad kid."

In situations in which you've been unjustly criticized, try to respond confidently and firmly while you communicate valuable and constructive information to the other person.

Hint: Words like "never" and "always" should be eliminated because upon examination, you will see that in most interpersonal contexts, these words are seldom true.

Sometimes partners expect their mates to read their minds and they are disappointed. A common case is one in which a woman feels angry and deprived because she expects her partner to suggest weekend entertainment plans. He, on the other, modeled himself after his father who left social plans to mother. A clear case of misunderstanding because of a lack of communication. Follow this scenario:

He: "You seem upset. What's wrong?"

She: "You never make any plans for the weekend. Don't you care to go out?'

He: "I didn't realize you wanted to go out since you haven't mentioned it. I thought you were content to hang out at home with our new big screen TV. Now, that I know how you feel, let's make a plan. Where would you like to go?"

This is an ideal solution to a simple misunderstanding.

**"He doesn't share his feelings with me. Sometimes I wonder if he has any."**

When your partner doesn't share, it may be that past experience has warned him to expect a negative reaction from a significant other. Perhaps he is hurt or angry about something you said and fears you will defend your position without taking his feelings or ideas into account.

When people are invested in being right, they do not listen to the other person's point of view, but concentrate instead on justifying their viewpoint.

Why is being right so important? Aren't you on the same team? An investment in being right is unprofitable and runs counter to a good relationship.

Communication is not a debate. It is not about winning or losing points.

Again, imagine yourself in your partner's place. How would you feel in her situation? Verbalize it: "I think I understand how you must feel."

It is gratifying to be understood and appreciated. It fosters intimacy.

To make sure you really do understand and aren't assuming something that may not be true, pose a question: "When I spend time with Tom, does it may make you feel I prefer his company to yours?"

You may learn from her response that it isn't the time you spend with friends, but that she considers Tom a heavy drinker and a bad influence on you. This will open a new dialogue. Reserve judgment and consider her points. Address her concerns without rationalizing your friend's behavior.

**"You should realize how tired I am and not pile more tasks on me."**

When you assume that your partner knows how you feel, you behave as though he can read your mind. As a result, your relationship suffers. You must clearly communicate what you want and how you feel in order to achieve emotional intimacy and harmony.

## Assumptions and Over-Reactions

Be alert for times when you may overact to your partner's behavior and as a consequence, you make false assumptions. Recognizing it, is your first step. The next step involves your apology. This costs you nothing and may be well rewarded.

Hint: Communicating your concerns should not drive a wedge between you.

To avoid this, begin your sentence with "I." For example: "I felt upset when you made the lunch date with your old girlfriend without discussing it with me."

It will bring a more positive response than: "You had no right making a date with your old girlfriend before discussing it with me."

## Arguments

In the heat of the moment, when arguments erupt into a shouting match and you have stopped listening to each other, it's best to take a break—a time out to re-think the disagreement and how best to resolve it.

Too often we take things too seriously and act as though a current problem is a life-threatening event. At such times, we need to disconnect and distance from it.

If you and your partner frequently laugh at the same things, you are very fortunate. This may be a good time to lighten up and counter harsh feelings with humor. *WARNING: This doesn't work with all couples.*

Remind each other about your pact to communicate openly and honestly and that you are partners willing to work on the problem to effect a mutually acceptable solution.

## Conflict Resolution

The mutual goal of conflict resolution is to effect a solution to a problem situation in which both parties have different and equally strong opinions, but are willing to use a valid method to resolve their conflict. They take turns in presenting their viewpoints without interruption.

When both parties are ready, they start by flipping a coin to decide who presents first.

### The Role of the Presenter

- To respectfully make only relevant and clear points and suggest a solution.

- Begin your sentence with "I": "I feel", "I think", or "It upsets me when" then present your viewpoint.

- Avoid words such as "never" or "always." These words are used in the context of blame.

- Do not blame the other person or make derogatory remarks about his friends or members of his family. He is not responsible for their behavior.

## The Role of the Listener

- To listen carefully to the other person's position without interrupting, no matter how tempting your rebuttal. Concentrate instead on what is being said. Reserve judgment until given sufficient time to fully absorb your partner's points and your partner indicates s/he is finished.

- To show you understand, summarize your partner's salient points.

- If you agree with the solution, congratulations!

- If you don't agree with the solution, ask for additional information or clarification.

Next it is the listener's turn to take the role of presenter. The presenter follows the strategy as described above and presents his or her solution to the problem.

The couple may need to go back and forth a few times to negotiate an agreement. They must remember that the goal is to treat each other's viewpoints respectfully and appreciate their partner's rationale.

Rarely is there only one solution to every relationship problem. They are urged to think creatively.

If anyone grows impatient, its time to call a time-out. The need for a time-out must be respected. Keep in mind that this task must result in a win-win solution.

Be patient with yourself and your partner.

Communication and conflict resolution skills require practice. Old habits are hard to break. Remember that you chose your partner for the good qualities you perceived. Mention these qualities as often as possible when appropriate situations arise. They are welcome gifts to give and to receive.

The following is a good example of how one couple used conflict resolution skills to solve their problem:

### Miranda and Max

Miranda, a part time physician and Max, a scientist, a couple in their early forties, married ten years, are parents of two young children. Sharing chores was the first difficulty the couple experienced early in their marriage, but they were able to compromise and enjoy life together.

Max grew up in a wealthy family with servants. Household chores were alien to him and he refused to do them. Miranda was disappointed because she had an unrealistic expectation that she and Max would do chores together, easing the load, just as her parents had done with each other.

To make peace, she agreed with Max's plan to employ a maid. It meant eating out one less time each a week. It was their first compromise together—a tool they would need in the future.

Harmony prevailed until the children were born and a problem with sharing parenting chores and juggling schedules emerged, but this time it loomed larger and there appeared to be no room for compromise.

It's important to note that Max and Miranda had distinctly different childhood backgrounds. His mother, a socialite left him in the care of a warm, but unobtrusive nanny. His father traveled worldwide for his business and spent little time with him.

Miranda' s mother was a stay-at-home mom while her father worked in his studio attached to their home. They doted on Miranda, their only child.

Miranda is very invested in what she considers proper parenting. She prefers to spend much of her time with her children. When she is not at the clinic, she helps out in the children's classrooms.

When her professional duties conflicted with her time with her children, she demanded her husband leave work to take care of them. She has fond memories of her father who found it easy and fun to do this. Miranda expected that Max would enjoy the rare chance to skip out of work be with the children.

However, Max's work situation is different from her dad's. Unlike her father, Max has the responsibility of supervising a team with a tight deadline schedule. He regards it unprofessional to leave work to collect his children from school. He prevails upon a willing neighbor, the mother of their children's friends to do it and supervise them until he or his wife returns.

Miranda accuses him of shirking his parental responsibilities. She believes that parents provide the best care, not surrogates such as child care workers, or neighbors. Max wanted to hire a nanny, but Miranda was adamant in her refusal. "I didn't have kids to have someone else raise them," she states.

She is critical of Max's laissez-faire parenting style and is angry that he has never read a parenting book. Max doesn't enjoy reading and he disagrees with her hovering over the children. He feels Miranda is overprotective. They have quarreled constantly because of what he perceived as her inordinate demands and his refusal to meet them.

Max connects his chronic headaches to these battles. He feels ridiculed by Miranda, and takes the opportunity to stay longer than necessary on out of town conferences, to avoid going home. This furthers disharmony at home. He seriously considered a physical separation, leaving child rearing entirely to Miranda.

Firmly convinced that her demands on him to parent according to her style were correct, she nevertheless became anxious about his wish to separate and the couple sought marital therapy.

This is what you can learn from their process:

They agreed not to act like opponents fighting a battle, but to be teammates with the common goal of preserving their relationship and finding a solution together.

1.  They sat down quietly, faced each other, without interruptions from radio, TV or phone calls. In this case, when the children were safely asleep.

2.  The presenter described his or her view of the problem without interruption by the other and suggested a remedy.

3.  "The listener," allowed himself to open up and truly hear the other person without planning a rebuttal.

4.  They examined their expectations of each other and determined together if these expectations were realistic.

Miranda learned that in order to achieve harmony at home, she would have to change her unrealistic expectations of Max. While her desire to provide the children with the best parenting is commendable, she had to accept that even experts disagree on parenting methods.

Max and Miranda looked at their roles differently— she from the eyes of a child of doting parents, and he from the eyes of a child of disengaged parents, each feeling comfortable with their childhood memories. When they shared this, they began to understand the roots of their problem.

Max's parenting style was not wrong, just different from Miranda's. He played with his children, but not often enough to suit Miranda. He spent weekend mornings playing basketball with his buddies. She thought he was selfish in wanting to meet his needs before meeting the children's, because it was not something she would do. She had to accept that Max was not her clone, and that love is a quality not a quantity. He loved his children, but didn't express it in her style. He expressed it as his father did, by working hard and putting as much money in their trust accounts as he could manage to insure a comfortable financial future for the family.

Max explained that his priorities were flexible. He needed to exercise and then relax with his buddies before spending time with his family. He agreed without any hesitation that in an emergency or a planned family vacation he would forgo the weekend routine Miranda had found objectionable.

While she would have preferred he felt the same way she did about the kids, she would have to accept him "as is" or bear the consequences of a marital separation.

Max discussed her hovering over the children. "You don't give them room to breathe."

Miranda assumed all children enjoy lots of attention. She just didn't know how to quantify it. She learned that ten minutes playing tag with Dad may be more fun than spending all day under Mom's constant surveillance.

When she learned that her excessive attention could cause a delay in the children's becoming self-reliant, Miranda began to back off.

To compromise, Max agreed to read parenting books and together they would discuss their respective opinions. Max did not keep his compromise to read the books, but he did find more time to engage with the children in the absence of Miranda's urging and fault finding.

To preserve the marriage, Miranda agreed to assume the primary responsibility of child rearing, and has hired a weekly cleaning crew to ease her burden.

| **6** | **Challenging Situations** |  |
|---|---|---|

The following scenarios present potential conflicts for couples.

Although some of these situations may not apply now, imagining how you would respond under these circumstances demonstrates your communication and conflict resolution skills.

Take turns answering these questions, using the lessons you've learned from the previous section.

1. You and your partner have planned an elaborate evening on the town. You've booked hard to get dinner reservations, and bought expensive tickets to the symphony. An hour before you are due to meet, you receive a call breaking the date because an old friend arrived unexpectedly from out of town and this evening is the only time they could see each other. How do you react?

2. Your mate loves a bargain. When complimented for an article of clothing she wears, she says she bought it on sale. This embarrasses you. You buy things regardless of the price. You consider comparison- shopping undignified. She is fiscally prudent and you are carefree. You have no savings and have been in debt. How would you handle the differences in your money management style?

3.  You feel uncomfortable when your partner turns his head to stare at other women, what would you do?

4.  Your partner continues a friendship with a former lover. They call and e-mail each other often. Occasionally, they go to lunch together. You feel threatened. How would you handle it?

5.  Your partner has a close friendship with a couple with whom you are uncomfortable. She frequently invites them to join your dinner dates. They talk about things they did in the past and people you don't know. How would you handle this situation?

6.  In competitive activities, your partner is invested in winning and rubs your nose in it. When you tell your partner this annoys you, he says he was only joking. How would you respond?

7.  Your partner sends mixed messages regarding sex. She is playful and affectionate, tickling and hugging you. This arouses you and when you attempt sex, she says she isn't ready. How would you cope?

8.  Sexual drive may change over time. One partner prefers more frequent sexual contact or one prefers it in the morning and the other at night. How would you accommodate?

9.  You have been offered a job promotion with a generous wage increase, a relocation expense package, and chance to rise quickly in the

company, but the new location has a harsh climate and you and your mate have a close support system of friends and family where you are now. The promotion would mean your mate would have to find work in this new state. Given her/his profession, it should not be too difficult.

10. You are eager to take this exciting new position. The offer could provide enough money for your spouse to stay at home and start a family. What steps would you take before making this decision?

11. Your future in-laws are meddlesome. They tell you where to shop, how to dress, and what kinds of gifts to give family members. You are concerned that they will rule your life. How would you handle this situation?

12. Your mother-in-law is rude to you and hurts your feelings. Your spouse doesn't stand up for you. What should you do?

13. Your partner has 50% custody of her young children from a previous marriage. What role do you expect to play in the children's lives in terms of supervision, discipline, support and protection?

14. One partner is a "neat freak" and the other is disorganized. How will you manage?

15. You are a new parent. Your spouse expects you to share childcare duties, but you aren't up for the task. Your demanding job leaves

little time, energy and patience. What do you do?

16. Your mate's brother is a recovering addict with multiple problems. She feels sorry for him and wants to take care of him until he is employed. Note: You can substitute aging or ill parents in this scenario.

17. You and your partner have heavy work schedules with little free time. You want to spend time together, but you also want time alone or with your friends. How do you juggle your schedule to meet your needs?

18. When you converse with your partner or other people, your partner often interrupts you. You feel disrespected. How do you manage the situation?

19. Your spouse in unexpectedly unemployed. The loss of income will impact on your lifestyle. How will you cope?

20. You have learned your mate has been unfaithful. What do you do?

| 7 | Suggested Solutions | |

There is more than one solution to most problems. Below you will find suggestions to the conflicts listed in the preceding chapter. It may be useful to compare each partner's answers with these. The solutions for every couple may differ. What is important is what works best for the couple. A few case studies demonstrate how actual couples found their way.

### Problem #1: The Lost Evening Out

You and your partner have planned an elaborate evening on the town. You've booked hard to get dinner reservations, and bought expensive tickets to the symphony. An hour before you are due to meet, you receive a call breaking the date because an old friend arrived unexpectedly from out of town and this evening is the only time they could see each other. How do you react?

### Suggested Solution

It's natural to feel disappointed in your partner's priorities. You may feel that she disrespected your feelings given the special plans and expenses you've made.

Many people would regard this as a valid concern to be addressed in your next meeting without delay. To ignore a partner's objectionable behavior, is unhealthy for the relationship. It gives your partner license to maintain that behavior. A relationship works best when you respect each other and yourselves.

As a practicality, you can use the reservations and tickets for yourself and an available friend, neighbor or co-worker, or go alone to dinner and try to sell the extra ticket at the concert hall.

Offering your partner the reservation and tickets sends a message that it is okay for you to be disregarded, and that you feel her priorities are appropriate. Do you think this is true?

If the situation were reversed would you break a well planned for date with your partner in order to see an old friend who suddenly springs from out of nowhere for an immediate visit with you?

### Problem #2: The Bargain Hunting Mate

Your mate loves a bargain. When complimented for an article of clothing she wears, she immediately says she bought it on sale. This embarrasses you. You buy things regardless of the price. You consider comparison- shopping undignified. She is fiscally prudent and you are carefree. You have no savings and have been in debt. How would you handle the differences in your money management style?

### Suggested Solution

Money is a topic of conflict for many couples. One may complain that his mate is a spendthrift. His mate complains that he is stingy. In most cases, an objective observer would consider their portrayal or each other as accurate.

It helps to learn what is behind each partner's characteristic way of handling money. In order to do this one must be willing to sensitively communicate a desire to understand the other. One must withhold any tempting remarks that blame or shame.

Exploring the subject in this way may lift the curtain drawn on emotional deprivation, or emptiness, so often a part of excessive spending.

Communication creates intimacy. It is vital to every aspect of your relationship. Taking each other for granted may create a feeling that something is missing in the relationship. What may be lacking is affection or attention.

It is perfectly fine on occasion to ask your partner if you provide enough attention or affection. It is important to tell your partner when you need more attention. Neither of you are mind readers.

Some people who feel deprived of attention and affection may over-spend to compensate. Sometimes it is conscious and deliberate. "He doesn't pay any attention to me, so I'll get even. I'll show him. I'll spend money on myself."

Overspending may be due to boredom. Shopping provides stimulation with the added excitement of acquiring new items to substitute for what you feel you are missing. Self-searching helps you to explore what it is that you lack and how you may attain or compensate for it in a healthy way.

If your partner readily admits shopping relieves her boredom, ask her if she would like you to make a suggestion. She may not want you to fix her problem, only to understand it. However, she must take responsibility for changing a habit that can adversely affect your relationship.

If she welcomes a suggestion, you can supply her with a list of places and things to consider as other sources of stimulation depending on her interests. These may include joining a book reading club, visit-

ing museums, art galleries, lectures, classes, or volunteering at a social service agency, an animal shel-
ter, a classroom or library. Ask her if she can suggest
an activity you can do together for recreation, such as
a sport, or a new hobby.

If the spendthrift follows through and sees some
value to avoiding shops and replacing the activity
with something fulfilling, it may help. If not, a "Shop-
pers Anonymous" support group may be available.

The stingy mate may have been raised in a family
forced to exercise caution in spending money because
of a precarious economic situation. Although his current situation may have improved, old habits are difficult to break. What he regards as a luxury, she may
regard as a necessity.

These matters can be explored and adjustments
made when couples are willing to sit down together,
listen carefully to each other and work as a team to
find a solution to the conflict. The key is to communicate early on before the situation gets out of hand.

### Holly and Howard

Holly and Howard knew their approach to spending money was different when they first met and began dating. Holly was prudent, always selecting the
lowest priced dinner on a menu while Howard paid
no attention to the cost of his meal. She bought mer-
chandise at reduced prices during sales, and clipped
coupons to save money at the supermarket.

When complimented on a new piece of clothing,
she would proudly announce she had bought it on
sale at a great saving.

Comparison-shopping was not in Howard's reper-
toire. When he saw something he wanted, he bought
it without considering the price or the possibility he
could find it for less elsewhere.

Their individual spending habits did not become
an issue until they married and pooled their money
into joint accounts. Howard's lavish spending style
began to arouse Holly's anxiety. He purchased everything he wanted, no matter the price without consulting Holly. He worked hard and earned a good income
and Holly did not want to deprive him, so she did not
voice any objection.

Holly tried to ignore the dent in their account, but
her anger came out in other ways. She became less
responsive to his sexual advances.

This pattern became a vicious cycle. The more he
would spend, the less interest she showed in him.
The less she responded to him, the more he would
spend.

Finally, after he purchased an expensive new car
using funds from their joint account without first
consulting her, Holly became livid. Until then, Howard hadn't a clue that he had been doing anything
wrong.

Their discussion about finances was long overdue.

At first Holly blamed Howard entirely until she
learned that had she voiced concern early, Howard
would have cut back. He explained that having been
on his own for many years before his marriage, he
didn't realize how important it was to discuss costly
expenditures with his wife before making a purchase.
He agreed to do so in the future. He told her he would

like her to loosen up and impulsively buy something nice for herself without it being on-sale.

This kind of discourse led to a greater understanding and appreciation of each other.

They decided to have three checking accounts: "His", "Hers" and "Ours." They would each place 25% of their respective income into their own personal accounts to do with as they pleased and 75% in "Ours." The latter account required joint decisions before making purchases over one thousand dollars. Howard knew Holly was prudent and trustworthy. He told her that she was free to dip into the joint savings at will. Since there was a large disparity between their earnings, the arrangement was equitable.

To Howard's credit, he did not use the disparity of their wages to exercise power, as is common in troubled relationships.

### Problem #3: The Wandering Eyes

You feel uncomfortable when your partner turns his head to stare at other women, what would you do?

### Suggested Solution

Frame your comment in a non-accusatory way: "Maybe you aren't aware of it, but when you turn your head to stare at other women, I feel uncomfortable. It's probably due to my insecurity and I need reassurance."

Many people sneak a peek at an attractive member of the opposite sex. It is like eye-candy for them. They may admire the person's appearance, but this does not mean they are comparing that person to you. You are not part of the equation.

Exposing your vulnerability to a mate increases intimacy. Your partner may continue this habit for awhile, but chances are, he will give you more attention because he feels closer to you.

### Problem #4: The Leftover Ex-Lover

Your partner continues a friendship with a former lover. They call and e-mail each other often. Occasionally, they go to lunch together. You feel threatened. How would you handle it?

### Suggested Solution

With a loving partner, there is no room for shame. If you feel ashamed of being jealous of your mate's former boyfriend, tell her. You want her to understand your feelings and to offer you reassurance.

Be specific. Tell her you feel threatened by their on-going phone calls, e-mail and lunch dates.

If she acts defensively, you may have a valid reason to feel threatened.

Explain that the contacts between her and her ex suggest her inability to let go of him. Tell her that it is uncomfortable for you, but you can understand how she may feel, and that you hope the good qualities in your relationship should help her overcome her feelings for her ex.

Such a conversation expresses concern for her feelings. This should open up her appreciation of how you feel. This kind of dialogue can go a long way toward achieving emotional intimacy. The two of you must come to the realization that past intimate relationships have no place in the present and intrude upon your building a life together.

## Problem #5: The Callous Couple

Your partner has a close friendship with a couple with whom you are uncomfortable. She frequently invites them to join your dinner dates. They talk about things they did in the past and people you don't know. How would you handle this situation?

## Solution

Some people are insensitive to others. This small group of people with a shared history, which they relive when together, may not be aware that they are excluding you from the conversation. It is easy for you, a newcomer to feel like an outsider.

At the first opportunity, change the topic by opening a new one. Talk about current events, sporting events, a movie you've seen, or a book you've read, or tell a joke or an anecdote. See if that helps dispel your discomfort.

You may have to do this several times for matters to change. If you continue to feel left out, tell your mate how you feel and suggest she join that particular couple without you.

## Problem #6: A Poor-Sport Spouse

Whenever you and your partner are engaged in a competition such as a board game, or a sport, he delights in winning and rubs your nose in it. When you tell your partner this annoys you, he says he was only joking.

How would you respond?

## Suggested Solution

If your partner enjoys competing with you, but you don't enjoy it, express yourself. "I don't enjoy competition. It's fun playing games, but it doesn't matter to me, who wins. It's just a game. I'd appreciate it if you would lighten up about it."

## Problem #7: Attention vs. Foreplay

Your partner sends mixed messages regarding sex. She is playful and affectionate, tickling and hugging you. This arouses you and when you attempt sex, she says she isn't ready. How would you cope?

## Suggested Solution

Couples learn sex cues from each other. A shoulder rub, a kiss on the cheek, or a hug may be a prelude to sex relations. The other partner gets the cue and responds with something akin to "Let's head for the bedroom." Each couple learns to give cues and to respond in their own style. Affection may or may not be a prelude to sex. Many people enjoy affection without sex. Others are rarely affectionate except during sex. You learn this as you experience each other. If you are easily aroused and your partner isn't, you can learn how to accommodate. An intimate discussion on what turns you on and off is important.

## Problem #8: Unsynchronized Libidos

Sexual drive may change over time. One partner prefers more frequent sexual contact or one prefers it in the morning and the other at night. How would you accommodate?

## Suggested Solution

Couples who share a similar degree of sexual drive are fortunate. When couples differ in the frequency of their desire, they can learn how to adapt to these differences.

To increase your libido (sex desire) pay attention to particular stimuli that arouses you. Sometimes when you're not in the mood, you can be aroused by certain stimuli such as sexy clothing, particular scents, dim lights, or music. A tender partner can learn how to excite you if you offer specifics as to what delights you sexually. If you don't view the big O as an absolute essential each time you have sex, you can please each other in many ways. Be imaginative and have fun.

### Problem # 9: Considering Relocation

You have been offered a job promotion with a generous wage increase, a relocation expense package, and chance to rise quickly in the company, but the new location has a harsh climate and you and your mate have a close support system of friends and family where you are now. The promotion would mean your mate would have to find work in this new state. Given her/his profession, it should not be too difficult.

You are eager to take this exciting new position. What steps would you take before making this decision?

### Suggested Solution

Many factors need to be considered before accepting a job promotion. Remember that unless your mate finds work quickly and is a resourceful, gregarious person, she will be alone during the day with no support system in place yet, as you will be at work. Neither of you may welcome her dependence on you for a social life. She may become resentful that you are able to socialize a bit with colleagues at lunch.

You and your mate must gather as much information as possible about the new environment and reach a mutually agreeable decision, taking into account all the factors. You can assign points to each item and then compare them with your current situation.

- Make a list of all the reasons to relocate. Visit the new job site, meet with co-workers and check out desirable neighborhoods in terms of cost, proximity to work and, conveniences.

- How does the real estate market compare with your present location?

- State the conveniences of the new town such as transportation, and other qualities you deem important such as schools, medical facilities, libraries, book stores, cultural and religious institutions, markets, cellular service if this important to you. (There are some out-of-reach areas of the country)

- Compare the cost of living with where you are now.

- How does the political, social and physical climate compare with your current location? Is it better or worse?

- How likely will your mate find satisfactory work in the new town?

- Examine what you will give up in order to accept the promotion. How important is your current support system of friends and family to you and your mate? How far away from your present location will you be?

Your goal is to reach a mutually agreeable solution. While a job promotion is desirable, consider the whole picture. You may be able to reach your career goal in your present location.

### Tina and Ted

Tina, an elementary school teacher was content with her work, old friends, and family life and had no desire to relocate. Her supportive large family lived nearby and pitched in when she unexpectedly needed help with chores, or children.

When Ted was offered a promotion at a new location three thousand miles away, she grew anxious. The promotion was important to Ted. It meant he could quickly rise up the corporate ladder and they would be in a better financial position. She knew Ted was ambitious and was eager to take the new job, but she had reservations. Because she didn't want to disappoint Ted, she agreed to visit the new location and gather information to help in their decision.

The town offered more cultural events, better schools, a transit system, and other conveniences. A gregarious person, Tina felt she and their pre-school children could adapt and make friends easily. Ted would make social connections at work. She could substitute teach in the school her children would probably attend until there was an opening for a permanent position. She could become independent from her family. She checked out the supermarkets and learned prices were somewhat lower. Real estate and gasoline were considerably cheaper.

Considering the lower cost of living and Ted's high salary, they could live in luxury and save money.

Tina talked herself into the positives of the relocation without considering any negatives. A native Southern Californian, she had not experienced harsh climate or cultural differences.

Ted realized Tina would miss her weekly visits with her old granny with whom she was very close. Tina's sister was due to give birth in a few months, and Tina wouldn't be available to help her as they had planned.

At the new job site, Ted had lunch with two men with whom he would have to work. They were cordial, but not forthcoming. He sensed some resentment and figured they had been in the running for his coveted position. The workplace atmosphere was more formal than what he was accustomed to, and he felt uncomfortable in the environment, but the promotion offered much more than his current salary. He thought of all he could do with the extra money.

Tina and Ted sat down, equipped with their lists, to evaluate the relocation plan.

Tina thought she could adapt to her new surroundings. She would find compensation for the loss of all she would leave behind in her husband's job satisfaction and in living a more luxurious life-style.

Ted knew that Tina was focusing on the positive in order to accommodate him. He knew her close friends and family ties were high on her list of priorities.

There are things money can't buy. No amount of money could compensate for an uncomfortable work situation and the loss of all they would have to leave behind.

With great relief, they decided that Ted would reject the job offer and remain in his present post.

He was welcomed back. Two years later when the director of his division retired, Ted was promoted to the position.

### Problem #10: Officious In-Laws

Your future in-laws are meddlesome. They tell you where to shop, how to dress for certain occasions, and what kinds of gifts to give family members. You are concerned that they will rule your life. How would you handle this situation?

### Suggested Solution

Meddlesome in-laws are invested in parenting and have trouble giving up the role. It may help to realize their behavior is well intended. They regard you as their child whom they love. Most emotionally healthy parents are pleased when their children find mates. They are eager for their children's contentment. It is best to thank your in-laws for their suggestions. You don't have to accept their suggestions unless you can separate the suggestions from the negative feeling you have being treated as a child.

### Problem #11: Rude Mother In-Law

Your mother-in-law is rude to you and hurts your feelings. Your spouse doesn't stand up for you. What should you do?

### Suggested Solution

Don't place an unfair expectation on your mate to stand up for you when his mother is rude to you. This problem is between your mother-in-law and you.

He loves both of you and cannot take sides unless he is offended by the way she speaks to you. In that case he can say, "Mom, it hurts me when you tell Donna that you think she's a rotten housekeeper. We both work and do the best we can."

If he is chooses not to complain to her, you must stand up for yourself. "It hurts me to hear you disapprove of my housekeeping."

## Problem #12: Previous Children

Your partner has 50% custody of her young children from a previous marriage. What role do you expect to play in the children's lives in terms of supervision, discipline, support and protection?

### Suggested Solution

Decisions about your role in the lives of your mate's children must be made together.

- What are her expectations?
- Do you agree with them?
- What are your expectations?
- Does she agree with them?
- When you observe her with her children, are you comfortable with her parenting style?
- What would you do differently?
- Discuss this with her.
- Are you at ease with her children?
- How do you feel about being an involved surrogate parent?
- How do you want the children to refer to you, i.e. Daddy Bob? Pop? What relationship would you like to have with her biological father?

## Problem #14: When Organizing Styles Collide

One partner is a "neat freak" and the other is disorganized. How will you manage?

### Suggested Solution

It is much easier for a disorganized person to cope with a neat person, than the other way around. A neat person has a profound problem in tolerating disorder. She can't help the way she is wired.

To a neat person, disorder is experienced much like a very loud noise blasting erratically.

Given the disorganized person's understanding of the very real problem of his partner, he can spare her from this unpleasantness, by comprising:

In areas that are used jointly, keep things in order. You may even begin to appreciate the value of order when items are easier to locate.

Confine your carefree approach to your own personal areas such as closet, drawers, office and personal car.

It works best when the neat person agrees to ignore her partner's haphazard personal space as long as she doesn't have to deal with it. Avoid asking her to locate something in your personal space.

## Problem #14: Becoming a Parent

You are a new parent. Your spouse expects you to share childcare duties, but you aren't up for the task. Your demanding job leaves little time, energy and patience. What do you do?

### Suggested Solution

If you don't feel prepared for childcare, explore your reasons. If you are afraid of the responsibility, explain it to your spouse. Perhaps you don't know how to care for an infant. Your spouse can teach you, or you can learn from short, easy to read, professionally recommended books on infant and child development. Infancy is a short period. Babies sleep most of the time and don't require constant attention. Toddlers require much more attention because they get into things and the house must be childproofed for safety.

It may be possible to accommodate your spouse by adding to your household chores on weekends, or hiring someone to help.

### Problem #15: Caretaking Extended Family

Your mate's brother is a recovering addict with multiple problems. She wants to help take care of him until he is employed. (You can substitute aging or ill parents in this scenario) You are concerned about how this will affect your life. How do you respond?

### Suggested Solution

Your mate's compassion and empathy for her family member is commendable. These qualities are important in building a future with her. To plan for the situation, you need more information:

- Does she expect her family member to live with you, or live nearby?

- Will he receive rehabilitation support services from a pubic agency to help ease his transition?

- What safeguards can be put in place to minimize a recurrence of his addiction?

- Does he have any skills that make him employable?

- What impact will this have on your family budget?

When the information is assembled, you will be in a better position to make informed choices to reach an understanding or compromise.

### Problem #16: Finding Enough Time

You and your partner have heavy work schedules with little free time. She wants more time with you. You want more time with her, too, but you also want time alone or with your friends. How do you juggle your schedule to meet your mutual needs?

### Suggested Solution

- If you work a reasonable distance from each other and it is convenient, have lunch together as often as possible.

- Connect briefly with each other on the phone daily.

- Schedule an uninterrupted time each day for a conversation. If you have no children, you can do this during dinner, otherwise at bedtime.

- Make a list of your free time and your priorities.

- Juggle your schedules according to these priorities.

### Problem #17: Conversation Interrupted

When you converse with your partner or other people, your partner often interrupts you. He doesn't do this with others, thus you feel disrespected. How do you manage the situation?

### Suggested Solution

Tell your partner when you have observed him talking with other people, he doesn't interrupt them, but when you are speaking, he often interrupts you. Ask him how he thinks this makes you feel. If he doesn't know, tell him that when he interrupts you, you feel insignificant, and disrespected.

Agree on a signal to use when he does this. The signal can be scratching your ear or humming a tune, or saying: "Excuse me, I haven't finished."

Although you are provoked, and tempted, avoid embarrassing him and yourself by commenting: "You're doing it again, always interrupting me. Never giving me a chance to finish a sentence."

### Problem #18: Unexpected Unemployment

Your mate is unexpectedly unemployed (due to illness, injury or business reverses) The loss of income will impact on your lifestyle. How will you cope?

### Suggested Solution

Adversity presents a challenge. Especially at this time you must offer your partner emotional support. Remember your priorities. You are a team. Express your love and affection and your companionship. Do not under any circumstance blame your mate. You are in this situation together and you must use your resources to cope with adversity.

Reorganization of your family budget may be needed. Find ways to economize: shop only for necessities and at discount stores, clip grocery coupons, learn to prepare quick, nutritious, inexpensive meals. This can be an exercise in creativity. Instead of expensive entertainment, you can play games, rent videos, listen to music, dance to old favorite c.d.'s, picnic in the park, visit friends, have pot-luck parties at home.

### Problem #19: Infidelity

You have learned your mate has been unfaithful. What do you do?

### Suggested Solution

It is very difficult to imagine how you would respond to this scenario after the initial shock. Most important is to consider the circumstances surrounding the affair.

- Were you getting along well?
- Were you or your mate under stress?
- Were you suspicious?
- Did you confront your mate with your suspicion or did he/she confess out of guilt?
- Was it a single event or an on-going affair?
- Did your mate deliberately seek the adventure?
- Was the experience meaningful to your mate?
- Was there something missing in your marriage? What was it?
- Are you and your mate willing to work on this?

As tempting as it may be, it is better not to ask for intimate details. This is counterproductive. The more you know about the other person, the more this person will intrude on your life.

- Have you considered your mate trustworthy until now?

- Does he appear genuinely remorseful for the pain he has caused?

- Is this the first time he has broken his vow of fidelity?

- If infidelity is a pattern, this behavior promises future pain.

| 8 | Case Studies of Personality Disorders | |
|---|---|---|

## "Doomed Relationships"

This section illustrates personalities that impact negatively on a relationship. Psychologists know that deeply ingrained personality disorders are unlikely to change without extensive therapy and even then, there is no guarantee. Such patients rarely stay in therapy long enough to determine if they can modify their behavior and dysfunctional belief systems that lead to chronic problems. People with these disorders have difficulty getting along with others, including therapists. We can describe these disorders and hypothesize about their origin, but despite scientific advances, as yet there are no sure-fire cures.

The individual with a personality disorder is bound to victimize those who allow it. It is important to be alert and not fall prey to the charisma, sex appeal and oft-times flagrant lies that people with personality disorders inflict on their victims. Oftentimes, the family members, business associates, and friends of people with personality disorders will seek psychotherapy or counseling for themselves, crying, "Help! She's driving me crazy!"

There is another type of personality, that of the hypersensitive person. This personality does not claim a psychiatric diagnosis, but it is worth mentioning because an intimate relationship with someone like this can be very stressful unless you're a highly tolerant person.

Hypersensitive people are overly alert to what's going on around them and have a keen sensitivity and an unpleasant reaction to strong noises, lights, certain foods, groups of people and the emotions and moods of others. They are afraid to take risks, usually avoid competitive sports, and may perceive many ordinary things as potentially harmful. They may get on your nerves because their feelings are easily hurt.

A highly sensitive person is a complainer, and never satisfied, as in the classic story The Princess and the Pea. You must be very patient and tolerant in order to get along with a hypersensitive person. You may have to tiptoe through life with such a partner.

However, on the positive side, you may find such people very interesting and refreshing because they are intensely in touch with good feelings such as love, joy and awe and find deep pleasure in the arts, literature and nature. They are never dull, and are exceptionally intuitive and artistic, but may not believe in their abilities. They have compassion and empathy for others and want to make the world a better place for all living creatures.

They can be charming and fun, but you must be prepared for their exaggerated misperception and response to their environment and to others. You must be able to step aside and detach from this person and refrain from saying, "That isn't the way I see it," because such a remark re-affirms what they already know—that they are different from others. As children their friendships were close and good, but their friends were those who felt different, too.

Remember your mantra: "I'm not a tailor and he's not a garment."

It is less painful to nip a toxic relationship in the bud than to spend years trying to work through difficulties causing frustration and resentment—especially when children are involved. Remember to say your mantra: "I am not a tailor and the person I want to change is not a garment."

The following are examples of difficult and oftentimes, unworkable relationships.

- The Stripper And The Speech Therapist: Sara And Craig
- The Hero And The Con-Artist Bob And Jill
- The Crazy-Maker Borderline Glenda And Jeremy
- The Paranoid Personality: Dennis And Hope
- The Hypersensitive Personality: Niki And Brian

## The Stripper and the Speech Therapist

A self-involved high-maintenance fiancée wears a danger sign, but the sign may be invisible to a person blinded by desire. In the throes of strong physical attraction or emotional need, the potential spouse may not realize early on that such a person will have unrealistic expectations of others. Such people are known as "narcissists" from the Greek Myth—Narcissus who fell in love with his own reflection.

### Craig and Sara

Craig was a young speech therapist assigned to a large elementary school district. He enjoyed working with children and helping them to improve their speech.

Sara was an assistant kindergarten teacher. He admired her tender, sweet manner with the children as she escorted them to his office several times a week. He was physically attracted to her and had frequent fantasies about her. She was tall and full figured and wore her long auburn hair tied back in a pony-tail. She had a wholesome, farmer's daughter look. A bit on the shy side, Craig couldn't bring himself to ask her out.

One Saturday, he ran into her at a shopping mall. He almost didn't recognize her. She wore a very short mini skirt and a thin camisole top. It was obvious she wore no bra. She invited him to lunch at a nearby café. Over coffee, she told him she was from a large family. She loved children and hoped to have a big family when she met the right guy. Craig was pleased to hear this. He too was from a large family and wanted to continue that tradition. Having this one value in common, he figured they seemed right for each other and began a relationship.

After a few months, Sara invited Craig to move into her condo. He was surprised she could afford such lavish quarters on her meager salary. She laughed as she told him she was paid well as an exotic dancer in a nightclub. She insisted that Craig watch her perform at the club. He had never been in a nightclub, but reluctantly, he complied.

Craig felt uncomfortable in that setting and told her he found it embarrassing to be around the scantily clad performers and the noisy men. Nevertheless, she demanded he continue to go in order to get over the embarrassment.

Craig returned to the club several times, sat alone and did not enjoy drinking and watching Sara's gyrations designed to arouse men in order to collect their money for her performance. He found it offensive. Craig preferred to think of Sara as the sweet, wholesome assistant teacher, clad in jeans and a loose shirt, her ponytail bouncing as she skipped with the children.

But when Sara wasn't at school, she dressed in sexy clothing. Her attire and seductive manner with other men made Craig feel uncomfortable, but he was afraid if he told her, she would be insulted and break up with him.

Sara couldn't seem to get enough of Craig. She insisted they drive to school together in her car even when he had after school conferences. She did not mind waiting and used the time to read romance novels. To assure his dependence on her, she advertised Craig's car for sale without first consulting him. When prospective buyers began to phone, Craig became angry at Sara's efforts to control him. For the first time in their relationship, he asserted himself and refused to sell his car.

Sara badgered Craig frequently about selling his car, but she couldn't make him change his mind. The car represented Craig's last vestige of independence and he would not give it up. She had a few temper tantrums, but did not threaten to toss him out.

Despite his concerns, Craig intended to marry Sara. He figured that once they had children, she would devote herself to them and she would give up her evening job.

Sara continued to complain about the few hours a week Craig worked out at a gym and for his unwillingness to sit at the bar and watch her perform. He offered a compromise: He would watch her performance once a week, if she would stop complaining about his workouts.

Sara refused to compromise. She insisted that he should cater to her to prove his love.

One day, the parents of a child in another school district contacted Craig requesting private speech therapy for their child. The referral could help start his private practice—his future goal. However, he did not discuss the job offer with Sara.

When she found out, she became enraged. "We don't need the money. I make enough," she screamed. "I want you here when I'm home. No gym. No extra work. Just you and me. Understand?"

Due to the escalation of her demands and arguments, the couple scheduled a psychological consultation. It was clear that Sara would not budge. She demanded that Craig do her bidding to prove his love for her. She thought her demands were justified and appropriate. She refused to accept that others could regard them as unreasonable and suffocating. Her narcissistic personality disorder was evident. She was self-absorbed and had unrealistic expectations of others. Her interest in children was superficial. Lacking empathy, Sara would boss them around and they would obey her. She showed no concern for the needs of others.

Craig soon learned that although physical attraction and the mutual desire for a family are important, they are insufficient for a wholesome intimate relationship,

## The Hero and the Con-Artist

A con-artist has an anti-social personality disorder. Many con-artists hold powerful positions in industry and government. Con artists are frequently depicted on nightly TV crime dramas, movies and novels. There is no available accurate information as to the percentage of our national population with this disorder. Immoral and unethical behaviors are not often reported and may not always constitute a crime. The anti-social personality usually presents a charming, engaging façade and is always on the ready to exploit others. Usually they prey on the vulnerable. Since most people are decent and have a conscience, they tend to judge others by using themselves as a gauge. Therefore, they are slow to pick up the clues. Such is the following case:

### Bob and Jill

Jill, a pert, vivacious, single, thirty-year old woman had her eye on Bob as he stepped out of a shining black Porsche in the parking lot near her apartment. She liked the cut of his expensive dark suit, his good looks and the way he carried himself. The heavy leather briefcase in his hand suggested that he was probably a successful lawyer.

On Sunday, she saw him again. This time he was relaxing near the swimming pool at the apartment complex. She glanced up from the pool at his fingers, looking for a wedding ring, but he wasn't wearing one.

Jill made her move. She pulled herself out of the pool near where he sat, and she smiled. "Hey neighbor, I'm Jill. I haven't seen you around. Are you new, here?"

Bob was taken aback by Jill's friendliness and her beauty— like a ray of sunshine in a gray day. She was the first person to show any personal interest in him since he had arrived from across the country. "I'm Bob. Just moved in last week," he replied. He was exhausted from relocating and having worked hard at his new job all week, but he perked up around her. He couldn't take his eyes off Jill's shimmering wet, tanned and toned body. "Do you like living here?"

She dried her sun-streaked blonde hair with a beach towel then wrapped the towel around her body. "Yeah, sure. Anyone sitting here?" she said, pointing to the chair next to him.

"Be my guest," Bob said.

Smitten with vivacious, attractive Jill, Bob was vulnerable. A newcomer, he was lonely, and in need of companionship and romance.

Very quickly, the couple became involved in a passionate love affair. Bob hoped their relationship would lead to marriage. He felt ready.

Within a month, Jill revealed she had lost her job and was in arrears on her rent. She told him she had no place to go. Without hesitation, Bob paid her back rent and invited her to move in with him.

The role of hero was one Bob enjoyed, and he was enamored with Jill. When Jill asked him for a loan to pay off her creditors, he rushed to her rescue.

He ordered a credit card in both their names and tried to teach her to budget, but Jill engaged in reckless spending, threatening his credit and made no attempt to find work.

Bob realized his relationship with Jill would jeopardize his professional and financial future, but he still had feelings for her and wasn't ready to turn her out. His dilemma caused him to experience depression and anxiety. Finally he sought psychotherapy.

After a few weeks, Bob reported that several small antiques were missing from his collection and Jill was his only suspect. Unable to trust and respect her, he decided to terminate the affair.

Good natured Bob rented an apartment for Jill several miles away. For a month, she stalked him. Bob was about to apply for a restraining order, when he learned Jill had moved, and had not provided a forwarding address. He figured she had probably found another vulnerable man to exploit.

In therapy, Bob quickly learned that his relationship with Jill was based on his vulnerability and loneliness as a newcomer, and Jill's exploitative nature. She had all the earmarks of an anti-social personality—a con artist. She took advantage of a single, lonely, good-natured and highly paid professional man ready and willing to come to her rescue.

Bob also learned that he could gratify his need to help others by volunteering in the community. Civic involvement restored his self-esteem and brought new friendships—friendships with people more like him.

## The Borderline Personality

In early childhood a pattern of unstable, intense interpersonal relationships unfolds for people with this disorder. Because their responses are unpredictable and impulsive, they often are described by those who know them as "crazy makers."

It is easy to be seduced when she claims you as a super-hero. However, later, and for no apparent reason, you suddenly become "good for nothing" or some other negatively described person. Her emotions run hot or cold and rarely lukewarm.

Such behavior may be marked by irritability, intense anger, temper outbursts, anxiety, suicidal gestures, excessive spending, sex, substance abuse, reckless driving, binge eating and undue suspiciousness attributing evil intent or inadequacy to others.

### Glenda and Jeremy

Glenda and Jeremy met during the second year of medical school. She was energetic, bright and charming, and he, although confident in his intellectual ability, had no confidence in his ability to attract women. When Glenda sought him out as a study companion, he was pleasantly surprised.

One evening after studying, Glenda unearthed an expensive bottle of wine. After they consumed it, she seduced Jeremy. It was his first sexual experience and he was hooked. After every study session, Glenda would produce another expensive bottle of wine. They would drink and enjoy passionate sex.

Glenda had a large supply of libido and expensive wine. After a month of this routine, her behavior abruptly changed. She accused him of sleeping with a professor—a woman who had praised him openly.

Glenda blamed Jeremy for withholding bits of information from her about a problem that they were studying. She said he was selfish because he didn't offer to pay for her weekly massage therapy visits. He had no clue that she had expected this from him. "I'm a poor medical student living off large financial loans," he explained. Glenda ignored his explanation. Frequently she would berate him over minutiae.

Jeremy's tolerance level began to fall and it took its toll during sex. When his anger affected his performance, Glenda screamed, "You're a queer."

"I don't need your abuse. I'm outa here!" he shouted, leaping out of bed. He quickly dressed then slammed the door behind him.

When Glenda called him a few days later inviting him to dinner, he had calmed down and accepted a ride back on her emotional rollercoaster.

Once, he overheard her arguing on the phone with her mother who apparently had accused her of spending money impulsively. Glenda promised she would cut down, but her lavish purchases continued. She accumulated a large wardrobe of clothes and jewelry inappropriate for a medical student's lifestyle. When Jeremy questioned her about it, she laughed and said her family was wealthy. They had homes in England and the United States and could well afford to pay her credit card charges.

Jeremy considered her expenditures impractical, but he realized it was none of his business, and he enjoyed being the recipient of her generosity in restaurants and in the bedroom.

However as time went on, he became increasingly alarmed by Glenda's heavy drinking and spending and her accusatory, irrational behavior. He decided to end their stormy relationship.

A few weeks later, Glenda called and explained, "I'm going through a bad patch with Mum. She is so selfish, strong willed and uncaring of my needs. She should appreciate how hard I'm working in med school. She accused me of stealing wine from the cellar. We've had a dreadful row. Why shouldn't I have the wine? It's mine, too," she said. "Everything in that damn house is as much mine as it hers."

"Seems to me, Glenda, you should have asked for it instead of just snatching it from your parent's collection," Jeremy said. "And maybe you are drinking too much."

Glenda became furious with Jeremy. She accused him of going behind her back to forge an alliance with her mother. Having never met her parents, he realized Glenda had made an illogical assumption and that she was irrational. "You're too off-base for me," he said, determined to finally end their tumultuous affair.

A few weeks passed. Glenda called Jeremy again and begged for his forgiveness. She blamed her behavior on her pre-menstrual syndrome. Jeremy, lusting for the sexual part of their relationship, couldn't resist her pleas and they resumed the relationship.

The pattern of instability continued. Jeremy couldn't predict or prepare for the changes in her behavior. When he suggested a mood stabilizer, she became enraged. "You idiot. You can't make a proper diagnosis. If it weren't for me helping you study, and that desperate professor you carried on with, you'd be tossed out of medical school by now."

For the final time, he slammed the door behind him, her insults echoing in his ears.

## The Paranoid Personality

Without justification, this person perceives the intentions of others as harmful. Distrusting, he is always on guard, reacting negatively to misinterpreted remarks. He suspects and fears exploitation and attacks and bears grudges indefinitely. This behavior may not come out immediately, but when it does, if you stay the course, you are doomed to an uncompromising, bumpy ride. No matter how clever you are, you cannot reason with an unreasonable person.

### Dennis and Hope

Loneliness and isolation struck Hope a month after her break-up with Rod, her fiancée. She had finished a few chores earlier than expected and wanted to go out and have fun, but her friends were busy, having made previous engagements.

Hope had stopped being disappointed in expecting Rod to choose her over a new job out of state. He'd wanted her to join him, but she refused. She enjoyed her current friends, her job, her colleagues and her condo and living in a warm climate. She didn't want to give all that up to be with Rod in an unknown situation. Hope didn't want to depend on one person for everything.

Rod had been right. He was usually right. If she truly loved him, it wouldn't matter so much where they lived, they'd have each other and would prevail. Certain about her decision, she realized she didn't love him. She didn't miss Rod. She missed having a relationship.

Hope headed over to the nearby tennis club. Upon her arrival, she was linked up with a partner to play doubles. The partner was Dennis; tall, dark, handsome, and as she quickly found out—single. Equally matched, they played well together. After a few hours of tennis, he asked her to dinner.

Over chilled margaritas, she told him about her recent engagement and how good she felt about her decision to remain in the area.

When questioned about his life, Dennis was hesitant at first. Finally, he revealed that he was over forty, never married, and had been an executive in a biotech firm from which he took an early retirement. His passions were tennis, surfing and running marathons.

Dennis had a pleasant smile, a good sense of humor, and with his athletic form, Hope found him physically appealing.

In a matter of weeks, they were inseparable. Although she thought Dennis was overly competitive and a big complainer; arguing about his scores with whomever he played, he was intellectually stimulating. She had never met someone as intelligent, well read and with such as vast fund of information. He seemed to be right all the time. Just like Rod. Only Rod never insisted that he was right. Dennis had to make the point that he knew more than others did about many things and that he was remarkably intuitive. In fact, he knew that she was still interested in Rod.

"That is absurd, Dennis. If I were interested in Rod, I'd be with him, not with you."

"Don't you dare say, I'm absurd." His face turned into an angry scowl, frightening her.

"I didn't say you were absurd, Dennis. I said the remark was absurd."

"I know what you meant," he said through clenched teeth.

"How can you possibly know what is in my mind?"

"I told you I'm intuitive. Don't you listen? I know you're still involved with him. You'll see him the first chance you have. Every time your line is busy, I know you're talking with him."

"You're wrong!" Hope's frustration grew as the argument escalated. Finally, she said, "I'm tired of trying to prove things to you. Can't we just change the subject?"

"No. Just get the hell out of here!"

Hope stormed out of the tennis club.

From that day on, at the club, Dennis ignored her greetings and treated her as a stranger.

Later, she learned that Dennis had been forced to retire because he had accused colleagues of stealing his ideas, and he was impossible to get along with because he was unforgiving, vindictive, highly competitive and suspicious of the motives of everyone with whom he had contact. Dennis was litigious, suing a long list of people he thought had cheated him.

## The Hypersensitive Personality

A close relationship with a hypersensitive person who misperceives the intentions of others and overreacts to situations can be enormously stressful unless you're a highly tolerant person.

## Brian and Niki

Brian, single at 36, was a career counselor at a community college where he met Niki, a 34 year old, bright, attractive woman who sought his help to find a suitable career. She'd been told she was a talented artist, but didn't believe it and was afraid to pursue it because the field was too competitive. He saw right away she was risk aversive which he'd have to keep in mind when going over her career choices. She'd had several disappointing low-level clerical jobs she described as exploitative. Niki felt unaccepted by her co-workers, but made friends with an immigrant woman who'd fled from a country unfair to women. Niki felt sorry for her and helped her learn the language and customs. Niki's compassion for this woman warmed his heart.

Niki took a battery of tests. The results showed a high intellect, cultural and artistic interests, empathy and a concern for the environment. He suggested several fields, but none sparked her enthusiasm. He felt challenged by and attracted to her. After he had completed his work with her, he asked her out

Brian found Niki intellectually stimulating. They shared a passion for many of the same things and for each other and became lovers. Because she fascinated him, he was able to ignore her frequent and numerous complaints about small stuff like an unbearable odor in a theatre, or the horrible noise of the air conditioner, or an insulting store manager, or being ripped off by her mobile phone service. Her complaint list was as long as his arm.

When she over reacted to something, he managed to push it aside, but when the frequency of her complaints started to annoy him, she sensed it and blurted out, "You're angry at me. I'm no good and you know it. I always say or do the wrong thing."

"I'm not angry at you. I'm sorry you get so upset," he said.

"No, you are angry at me. I'm a terrible person and you know it."

Her exaggerated reactions had put him on guard and realizing further words would inflame rather than calm her, he kept silent.

"I'm going back to my crappy apartment. That's all I deserve," she said and stormed out.

Brian wondered whether the excitement and pleasure he felt with Niki was worth her annoying complaints and her over-reactions. He decided to hang in there and let time tell.

When Niki's clerical job ended due to outsourcing, she had a "meltdown." Furious at the country's economic policies and corrupt corporations, she rambled and raved non-stop about it. Trying to soothe her, Brian listened and stroked her hair. He enjoyed trying to calm her and was often good at it. At times she expressed doubt over his feelings for her, but he wasn't going to propose marriage until he knew her long enough to see if they were right for each other. Given her aversion to risk, she would likely decline and he wasn't ready for her rejection.

One evening over dinner at a crowded restaurant, in response to Niki's job search complaints, Brian suggested social work as a possible career move. When he saw the look of horror on her face, he realized he should have kept quiet. She was already uncomfortable, sneering at the noisy people at nearby tables.

"Stop trying to manage me," she shouted, before bolting from the restaurant.

Brian attributed her behavior to the frustration she was experiencing and her inability to cope with it, so he promptly paid the check and found her sobbing outside. He gently reached for her hand. Niki was lucky to have hooked up with a supportive, understanding and patient person, but time will tell if the relationship will last.

### Summary

These case studies illustrate key enduring, inflexible personality elements that form a pattern not readily broken. Such personality characteristics inhibit social and occupational functioning and must be considered when faced with a decision as far-reaching as marriage.

A successful, comforting marriage depends on much more than physical attraction and the sharing of similar interests and hobbies. You must also have the same values and goals, to accept that you can't change your mate and you must be willing to accommodate, to reach compromise and to feel that you are on the same team.

| **9** | **People You May Meet** |  |
|---|---|---|

Hopefully, you're among the fortunate to have connected with your mate on a deep emotional level and are ready to commit to shared values and a life-long companionship, to be there for each other through joy and sadness. You agree to accept each other's imperfections, and to work out any difficulties that occur between you now and in years to come. By now, you have developed skills to help you in this process, and if not, you are open to learning. You understand that you won't always be able to meet each other's immediate needs and that you must be self-reliant, yet confident that your partner will offer emotional support when necessary.

In the process of getting along with each other and your respective families, friends, and colleagues, it may help to have a basic understanding of the diverse personalities that may come your way.

### Old Souls

Some people are fortunate to have an inborn, deep understanding of themselves and of others. Often such a person is described as "an old soul." Such people have intuition and a keen insight of their assets and liabilities and a strong grasp on how to best function alone and with others. Such a person is most often the easiest to be around.

### Know-It-Alls

And there are those who enjoy showing off their fund of information about many things, science, technology, law, history and more. You may find them pompous and annoying. While they may be competent in navigating their world, and can nurture themselves, they haven't a clue about their effect on others. These people may show no need for intimacy. They are independent—self-contained, but as flawed humans, their imperfections may include poor manners. They often don't stop to think and consider their effect on others. They may insult, humiliate and annoy associates or family members. Perhaps they feel more comfortable being hostile and self involved and prefer to keep others at an emotional distance.

Needless to say, they make difficult mates, if perchance they happen to connect on a superficial level and somehow consider marriage a necessary expedient towards furthering their professional or career goals. Such a person may take the form of an in-law or other family member making an appearance at family functions. If such a person is important to your mate, you may have to make small compromises. If the family is large, you may be able to avoid being in his immediate proximity. Depending on your own level of tolerance, you can choose to limit or avoid discussions with this person. However you must respect and accept your mate's willingness to spare you discomfort by attending some of these functions without you.

Kim, a petite, soft-spoken woman, 4'10" weighing under 100 pounds had recently become engaged. Everything was going well until she met her prospective in-laws. She felt very uncomfortable with them. They are very different from her family and from the few people she's known. She regarded them as insensitive because they don't censor what they say. Her future brother-in-law Ted jolted her with loud, uncalled for remarks about her appearance, questioning why she was just "skin and bones." She felt embarrassed and overwhelmed. Ted is a huge man, over 230 lbs. and about 6' 5". Kim described him as a show-off, crude, and rude. She figures this must be the reason he is still single at 50 years of age. Because she felt uncomfortable, she lost her appetite, and barely touched the feast his family prepared.

Ted called attention to her at the table as she picked at the enormous amount of food his mother had placed before her. In an angry, obnoxious voice, he announced that Kim has anorexia and should get it fixed before she marries his brother. At first she was dumbfounded. Finally, she gained the courage to explain that many Asians like her are naturally thin and petite, and that she usually eats well and has complete physical exams yearly, in fact her doctor recently pronounced her healthy. She had hoped this explanation would end the discussion, but it did not.

Ted went into a huge lecture about anorexia and said he was certain of his diagnosis and that her doctor was ill informed. Ted is not a doctor. Kim decided a reply to him would only cause further distress, so she ignored his remark.

A little later, he questioned Kim's legal knowledge and snickered and sneered at her responses. Law is an area where Kim feels most competent having passed the bar the first time and earning a position at a well respected law firm. Nevertheless, she felt intimidated and under severe scrutiny by Ted.

Kim was in conflict. She loved her fiancé, but found his family intolerable. She decided to consult me. She opened with a description of the above events, following it with this question:

"I know if I marry my fiancé, I will have to be in the company of his family for the rest of my life, but the thought of it makes me ill. I don't expect him to defend me, because I prefer do that for myself. What should I do?

If you have connected with your mate on a deep emotional level and are ready to commit to shared values and a life-long companionship, consider that you won't be spending every moment of your life in the company of his family. You and he will be there for each other exclusive of them.

There may be several reasons that Ted was cruel to you. He may be jealous of your fiancé for having connected with someone as fine as you. Therefore, he must "put you down" to make you appear less than desirable in his own eyes or in the eyes of his brother, or to make you angry at him and thus prevent any attraction he may feel towards you.

My advice to Kim: if your mate's relationship with his brother is important to him and he feels deeply committed to attend all family functions, you may have to make small compromises. If the family is large, you may be able to avoid being in Ted's immediate proximity. You can choose to limit or avoid discussions with him. You don't have to force yourself to be in his company in order to please your mate. Discuss your feelings with your fiancé. Perhaps he will be willing to spare you by attending some of his family's functions without you. As a busy attorney, you will no doubt have reasonable excuses to keep you away from Ted's unpleasantness. In time, you may learn to accept the rest of his family, and even may find some endearing qualities in them.

### Over-Givers

There are some people who seem to care more about others than about themselves. They may deprive themselves to please others. Perhaps they may have felt unloved as children and don't feel entitled to love until they earn it by their good deeds. They may present you with gifts they may not afford, or be quick to volunteer for a task. Once you understand this characteristic, you may find this person easier to be around than the one described above.

### Short on Self-Esteem

Some people suffer from insecurity. They are overly sensitive and over react to the slightest hint of criticism. They have many "hot buttons" and suffer from profound self-doubt and expect failure and rejection in careers and relationships. They may set themselves up for defeat, almost as though they must prove their interpretations and expectations are correct. It is likely that in their tender years, they experienced rejection, abuse or neglect. Oftentimes being in their company can become very trying because they may falsely accuse you of criticism you hadn't leveled. The best way to deal with such a person is to simply explain your position and avoid prolonging the conversation. You can politely say, "I'm sorry you feel that way. It isn't my intention to offend you."

### Without A Clue

Surely, you will come across people who have no insight. They may behave in self-destructive ways and may surround themselves with contemptible people perhaps because they are familiar with that type person. They yearn to win the wrong person over, much as they may have tried to do, but failed with early figures in their lives.

Such a person will have little impact on you if you aren't involved. However, if someone close to you behaves his way, you can politely offer an explanation of what you think may be going on. For example: "I'm no shrink, but I've read that when people try to make the wrong person like them, it may because they're repeating what happened to them in childhood." There is no guarantee that this will work, but you may be giving him something to consider.

### Need To Handle Personal Issues First

Although psychotherapy is a significant, deeply rewarding experience, not everyone chooses to invest the time and money, unless they are troubled by emotional distress, or ready to embark on a quest for lasting self-improvement. Certainly anyone experiencing depression, anxiety, panic attacks, phobia, post-traumatic stress, inability to sleep well, struggling with conflict over a relationship or a job, or a distressing matter, would be well advised to seek professional attention recommended by a trustworthy source.

If you want to gain an understanding of yourself and others a variety of paths are suggested in the Appendix.

| Appendix | Recommended Resources | |
|---|---|---|

## Fiction

As children, the development of our values stemmed from our parents, our teachers and other important people in our lives, but also from the profound influence of the books we read. For example one of the major themes in the masterpiece *Great Expectations* by Charles Dickens is that the significance of life is not in one's material achievement or social status, but in integrity, loyalty, and honesty in relationships.

In the process of reading, or in viewing a film, we have a chance to identify with the characters and become aware of what makes them tick.

Books that impact the way in which people view themselves and their world are among the many favorites:

Angelou, Maya. (1968) *I Know Why the Caged Bird Sings.*
Cervantes. (1605) *Don Quixote.*
Dostoyevsky, F. (1880) *The Brothers Karamazov.*
Thoreau, Henry. (1854) *Walden.*
Tolstoy. (1869) *War and Peace.*
Twain, Mark. (1885) *The Adventures of Huckleberry Finn.*

Exploring literature can be enjoyable and increases your knowledge of humankind. You can learn about the classics in adult education classes, or on the shelves in your public library, and by online searches for classic literature with themes that provoke and enlighten you. An excellent resource is the Great Books Foundation, an organization that helps you join or start a discussion group (see www.greatbooks.org)

A comprehensive list of links to book reviews, book recommendation sites and text books in the public domain can be found online at www.refdesk.com/books.html

You can find full text versions of the classics at Project Gutenberg (www.gutenberg.org) and www.literature.org.

When couples read and digest the same book or view a film together, and they discuss it, the activity can help them learn more about each other on a deeper level. It helps foster and maintain intimacy.

## Non-Fiction

Of course, there are the standard self-improvement books. Many cited here are considered classics in the field written by highly regarded authorities. The books are listed alphabetically by the author's last name. You may find them on the shelves of your public library, or the librarian can order them for you at no charge. Online bookstores offer brand new and older editions or used copies of worthwhile books.

**Self-improvement books can be helpful, but remember, they are not a substitute for professional therapy.**

## Getting Along Well with Yourself and Others

Bach, S. (1970). *The intimate enemy.* New York: Avon.

Bach, S. (1970). *Pairing.* New York: Avon.

Beck, A. (1998) *Love is never enough: how couples can overcome misunderstandings and resolve conflicts.* New York, Harper Perennial.

Boles, R.N. (2007) *What color is your parachute: a practical manual for job hunters and career changers.* Berkeley, CA. Ten Speed *Press.*

Bronson, P. (2000) *What should I do with my Life?* New York, Random House.

Bronson, P. (2005) *What should i do with my life? The true story of people who answered the ultimate question.* New York, Random House.

Burns, D. (1999) *Feeling good workbook.* New York, Plume. An authority on cognitive-behavioral approach to anxiety, depression and panic any of his books can be helpful.

Ellis, A. (1975) *How to live with a neurotic:* New York: Crown Publishers.

Ellis, A. (2000) *The secret of overcoming verbal abuse: Getting off the emotional roller coaster and regaining your life.* North Hollywood, CA, Wilshire Book Co.

Ellis, A. (2006) *How to stubbornly refuse to make yourself miserable about anything.* New York, Citadel.

Ezrin, S. (2006) *Living through transitions: Harnessing your courage at a personal crossroads.* Toronto, Canada. Trafford.

Forward, S. (1989) *Toxic parents: overcoming their legacy and reclaiming your life*, New York Bantam Books.

Frankl, V. (2006) *Man's Search for Meaning* , Boston, Mass, Beacon Press. Note: Dr. Frankl, a concentration camp survivor, explains how he maintained his mental health during a horrific ordeal.

Greenwald, H. (1966). *Emotional Maturity in Love and Marriage* . New York: Atherton.

Greenwald, H. (1980) *The Happy Person: A Seven-Step Plan*, New York, Stein and Day

Lerner, H. (2001) *The Dance of Connection: How to talk to someone when you're mad, hurt, scared, frustrated, insulted, betrayed or desperate.* N.Y. Harper Collins (note: this is her most recent book, but her other books are also recommended.

Nowinski, J. (2001) *The Tender Heart, Conquering Your Insecurity* N.Y. Fireside Simon and Shuster.

Seligman, M. (2002) *Authentic Happiness and Learned Optimism,* N.Y. The Free Press

Seligman, M. (2007) *What you can change... and what you can't: the complete guide to successful self-improvement.* New York, Random House.

Carlson & Shield, Ed. (1995) *Handbook for the soul.* New York, Little, Brown and Company (essays on philosophies and creeds encourages introspection)

Wallin, P. (2001) *Taming your inner brat*, Hillsboro, Ore. Beyond Words Publishing. (A down to earth, easy read)

## Sexuality

Berne, E. (1973). *Sex in human loving.* New York: Pocket Books.

Comfort, A. (2003) *The new joy of sex series*, New York: Pocket Books (Note: there are many editions of this book in hardcover and paperback, any book by Dr. Alex Comfort would be helpful.

Lusterman, D.(1998) *Infidelity: a survival guide.* California: New Harbinger

Masters, W.(1974). *The Pleasure Bond.* Boston Mass: Little Brown.

Reik, T. (1957). *Of Love and Lust.* New York: Farrar Strauss Cudahy.

Schultz, D. (1984). *Human Sexuality.* Englewood Cliffs, N.J.: Prentice Hall.

## Sexual Addiction

Carnes, P.(2001) *Out of the shadows: understanding sexual addiction.* Center City, MN Hazeldon Publisher.

Penix, Sbraga and O'Donohue ( 2004 ).*The sex addiction workbook: proven strategies to help regain control of your life.* Oakland, CA. New Harbinger.

## Finances

Chatzky, J. (2003) *You don't have to be rich,* N.Y. Penguin.

Maranjian, S. (2001) *The motley fool money guide: personal finance, investing* (note: this book is updated periodically by Motley Fool Publishers).

Opdyke, J. (2004) *Love and money: financial fundamentals, building a life together, planning for the future*: N.J. John Wiley.

## Cinematherapy

Viewing and analyzing professionally recommended films can enhance personal growth. Not only are we entertained, but we can relate and identify with the characters. Their plight may resonate with us. This process is termed, "Cinematherapy." According to Dr. Birgit Wolz, "Cinematherapy allows us to use the effect of imagery, plot, music, etc. in films on our psyche for insight, inspiration, emotional release or relief and natural change." Some favorites:

*A Catered Affair* (1956): A powerful drama centered on wedding plans written by Paddy Chayefsky and Gore Vidal. Explores issues of personal finance, the relationship between parents, in-laws, family conflict, daughter-mother relationship.

*Marty* (1955) An award winning film, also written by Paddy Chayefsky (1955), offers a character study of two lonely, single people who triumph by their relationship.

*The Brothers McMullen* (1995): The intimate friendship and family bond allows brothers to be honest and open with each other while discussing their individual crisis. This film provides an excellent exploration of men's relationship with women.

*Love with a Proper Stranger* (1963): The traumatic consequences of a "one night stand" presents a good character study and view of family relationships.

*The Lost Weekend* (1945): A masterpiece about alcohol addiction.

*Sleepless in Seattle* (1993) exposes the difference between the view of love and romance within this particular couple.

*Twelve Angry Men* (1957): A powerful display of integrity of character in the quest for fairness.

*War of the Roses* (1989): A soon-to-be-divorced couple cannot agree on a property settlement and reveal their intense feelings by escalated, unremitting combat.

For a list of other films depicting specific themes that may have special significance to you, click on: Cinematherapy.com where you will find film descriptions, reviews, and directions for using films therapeutically.

## Watching Films: Guidelines for Self-Exploration

In preparation for each viewing session, sit comfortably. Let your attention move effortlessly, without strain, first to your body then to your breath. Simply inhale and exhale naturally. Follow your breath in this innocent, watchful way for a while. Notice any spots where there's tension or holding. As you grow aware of them, let your breath travel into these spots. To release tension you may experiment with "breathing into" any part of your body that feels strained. Never force your breath.

Your gentle attention is sufficient to help you become more present and balanced, as it spontaneously deepens and corrects your breathing if it is constricted. Experience your condition without inner criticizing or comment. If you notice yourself judging or narrating, simply listen to the tone of your inner dialog as you come back to your breath. Lay judgments and worries consciously aside.

As soon as you are calm and centered, start watching the movie. Most of the deeper insights arrive when you pay attention to the story and to yourself. While viewing, bring your inner attention to a holistic bodily awareness (felt sense). This means you are aware of "all of you"—head, heart, belly, etc. Once in a while you might notice your breathing from an inner vantage point—from your subtle, always-present intuitive core. Observe how the movie images, ideas, conversations and characters affect your breath. Don't analyze anything while you are watching. Be fully present with your experience.

Afterwards reflect on the following:

- Do you remember whether your breathing changed throughout the movie? Could this be an indication that something threw you off balance? In all likelihood, what affects you in the film is similar to whatever unbalances you in your daily life.

- Ask yourself: If a part of the film that moved you (positively or negatively) had been one of your dreams, how would you have understood the symbolism in it?

- Notice what you liked and what you didn't like or even hated about the movie. Which characters or actions seemed especially attractive or unattractive to you? Did you identify with one or several characters?

- Were there one or several characters in the movie that modeled behavior that you would like to emulate? Did they develop certain strengths or other capacities that you would like to develop as well?

- Notice whether any aspect of the film was especially hard to watch. Could this be related to something that you might have repressed ("shadow")? Uncovering repressed aspects of our psyche can free up positive qualities and uncover our more whole and authentic self

- Did you experience something that connected you to your inner wisdom or higher self as you watched the film?

**Hint: it helps to write down your answers.**

If some of the mentioned guidelines turn out to be useful, you might consider using them not only in "reel life" but also adapt them to "real life" because they are intended to make you become a better observer.

For a list of other films depicting specific themes that may have special significance to you, click on: Cinematheray.com where you will find film descriptions, reviews, and directions for using films therapeutically.

Excerpted with permission from www.CinemaTherapy.com by Birgit Wolz, PhD.

# Index

# For Counseling Professionals and Therapists